POETRY RIVALS 2012

STROKES OF INSPIRATION

Edited by Donna Samworth

First published in Great Britain in 2012 by:
Forward Poetry
Remus House
Coltsfoot Drive
Peterborough
PE2 9BF
Telephone: 01733 890099
Website: www.forwardpoetry.co.uk

Book Design by Spencer Hart & Tim Christian

SB ISBN 978-1-84418-612-9

FOREWORD

In 2009, Poetry Rivals was launched. It was one of the biggest and most prestigious competitions ever held by Forward Poetry. Due to the popularity and success of this talent contest like no other, we have taken Poetry Rivals into 2012, where it has proven to be even bigger and better than previous years.

Poets of all ages and from all corners of the globe were invited to write a poem that showed true creative talent - a poem that would stand out from the rest.

We are proud to present the resulting anthology, an inspiring collection of verse carefully selected by our team of editors. Reflecting the vibrancy of the modern poetic world, it is brimming with imagination and diversity.

As well as encouraging creative expression, Poetry Rivals has also given writers a vital opportunity to showcase their work to the public, thus providing it with the wider audience it so richly deserves.

CONTENTS

THE POEMS

IMPERFECTIONS

It's the imperfections that make us who we become
they will simply help us grow and make our spirit strong
some mistakes we make I know it happens now and then
which sometimes we forget about and then repeat again.

That's what makes us human no question about that
but if we hide what is within it makes us a spoilt brat
but what no one wants to know is all the silent tears
for that would mean admitting that they, too, have fears.

We try so hard to cover up those feelings deep inside
yet we know that our shining spirit will not be denied
it gives us strength and guidance as we go on our way
it helps us through the battles we're fighting every day.

We're judged by those around us for everything we do
they see the imperfections yet they don't have a clue
the potential of our being is far greater than they think
and if they really want to see it they only need to blink.

It's only when we go through life seeing what is real
that we accept our fears and open up to what we feel
with our eyes wide open see the truth is now revealed
and look beyond the attitude that acted as a shield.

Now the veil's been lifted and the mist has blown away
it will be so much easier to make it through the day
now we can let go prejudice and friendships can begin
as we share love that for so long was locked away within.

Monica Partridge

AGAIN OR A GAIN

In an age of unrest and upheaval
our world is in torment again
everyone's angry at someone
inflicting hatred and pain
as we stumble towards a conclusion
will our lives ever be here the same
or is this all an illusion
because nobody knows who to blame?
Some strive to grab all the money
some try to win every game
but me,
all I want is my Saviour
and to live up to Jesus' good name
there's so much love that's unheard of
and so much joy we could gain
if we put our hand in the hand of our Saviour
we'd never need worry again.

Daphne Cornell

TWO SPOONS

A friend of mine described me as a
'Bloody force of nature' and I feel it,
sometimes. Two spoons in my coffee cup.

He smirked about those girls, those girls
that *seem* 'normal' and how I'm one.
'Least you know it,' he said, '. . . force of nature.'

'You dance through life like smoke from a gun,
a gun that shoots weak-hearted men, you dance
them dead,' he said and I believe him.

Kiss off each one at platform 3. The spoons
outnumber us, Mark. I am who I have to be.

Natalie Rogers

WHEN HE ISN'T WATCHING

I get up to my tricks when He isn't there
When He isn't watching . . .
I do what I probably wouldn't
If I could see Him right there
I'm not that 'saintly'
I see how far I can go . . .
Do I test God?

I let the little foxes in sometimes
Do I allow them to destroy the vine?
Perhaps not
But . . . nearly,
When He isn't watching

But, who says He isn't?
He sees; He knows everything . . .
There's nothing I could hide from Him
Even if He wasn't watching
Is He really watching?

Anita Igboayaka

FLOWERS BY THE ROAD

They once stood proud in light of day.
But here they shed
their shades of red
to cast a shroud upon the way.

Though lost, they rise once more
with brighter leaf.
As hearts that grief
has rent again shall soar.

Steve J Waterfield

RELENTING VISIONS! NIGHT-TIME MISSIONS

Owls are hunting,
Eagles flying,
Slowly swooping, never landing,
Eyes are watching; nightly prying.

Staring; smiling; blanked out faces,
Teardrop masquerades dancing round,
Bellowing voices; unknown places,
Strangely drowning with the sound.

Climbing stairways,
On and upwards, never-ending,
A night-time causeway,
Fast descending,

Running marathons,
Breathlessly panting; hearts are pounding,
Night-time carnage; fighting garrisons,
Screaming motions; silently sounding.

Climbing mountains; night-time missions,
Relenting visions on downward slopes,
Falling! Calling! Wrong decisions,
Diminishing dreams; losing hope.

Dianne Audrey Daniels

TIME

The sands of time like an hourglass
Runs dry of sand every day for me
Not a tear for me do you cry
For time is passing me so quickly by
Soon my name you'll forget
Like the picture on the Wall
That looks pretty and very small
Is all that reminds you of me
A church, a Wedding
A beautiful bride, a handsome groom so smart
How happy times you long for now
If only it could be that way for me too
Time is running out you see
We are growing older every day
How I miss your company when we are apart
My heart is broken, it makes me sad
Counting our blessings every day
For every boy there is a girl
Wish you were that one for me
As not many are beautiful as you
So in love am I it pains me so
Each hour of the day I think of you
The hourglass is running dry
How quickly time has gone by
So time does quickly fly
How it makes me sigh, so sad to cry.

George Barr

DAD

He showed me the way, he taught me how to live life and to be free.
He never prejudged, he never controlled, he showed me how to be me,

Now time has gone by and he is no longer the person that I used to see,
For something has taken his spirit away and left him a shadow of what he used to be.

He wanders around in a place full of people, he hardly knows they are there,
He can't do that much for himself anymore, he would die in this world without care.

But he is still here, I saw in his eyes the man that I once knew,
Just lost and alone, living a life so different to me and to you.
He looks at my face and he knows who I am as then he begins to smile.
And we are together, father and son, if only for a short while.

We will have a small chat, about what I don't know, I will share some pictures and tea.
And then we will hug as I turn to go and he returns to his world without me.

He showed me the way, he taught me how to live life and to be free.
And no matter what happens in his life or mine, he will always be special to me.

Adam Crawley

SPLIT INFINITIVE

To be
or not to be/or to be not?

Her decision: At breaking point, life – brittle as a lead pencil
she is hopelessly trapped/trapped hopelessly.

No forward. No back.

Stock still, she listens intently/intently listens for answers to her prayers but
only hears/hears only the wind and rain in the dark.

God-fearing, she fears infinity – what if there is no end?
What if it is a mortal sin to not be/to be not?

Split road ahead –
She sits infinitely still, still infinitely.

Sharon Lansbury

BROCCOLI IS A POLITICAL STATEMENT

Give peas a chance,
Make peas, not war,
Broccoli is a political statement,
The carrots are what we are fighting for.

Our freedom lies in sweetcorn,
The potato is our friend,
Asparagus says 'no' to oppression,
Swede is the beginning and the end.

Vote with your spoon
And protest with your fork,
Leave the knives to the hooligans,
Save your lives from the hooligans,
Let the mushrooms talk.

Eat local, act global,
Wave a turnip at the factory farm.
Raise the alarm,
Don't stay calm,
The people are starving
Whilst we feed all the crops
To the cows.

Now
Is the time to let broccoli be
A political statement.
Respect the animals,
Respect the people,
Wake up to the compassion
In you.

Nicole Peake

THE SUN'S POWERFUL RAYS

The heat has caused the tar,
Upon the road's surface,
To bubble up and act like fly paper,
Trying to attach everything,
That has cause to pass over,
The poor roses,
Which the gardener was once so
Proud of,
Now hang their head in shame,
With petals now turning brown,
They glance upon the ground,
From which they came,
Dazing rays blind the unshielded eyes
Like the furnace flame,
It takes delight,
As it burns the naked flesh,
While the mere mortals,
Pray for any breeze,
Which the wind might send,
Cattle seek the shade,
Of the overhanging trees,
That line the hedges
Along the fields in which they graze,
Blessed are these summer days,
And long many wish they would stay,
For there are those who worship,
And embrace,
While others stare in awe,
As they ooze from every pore,
Wondering why they don't melt away
They can not understand the fools,
Who try to imitate,
And suffer for their sin
Those who worship the sun,
They just lie there and burn.

Pauline Uprichard

RADIO REQUEST!

A woman's voice on the radio today, truly made me weep,
Her heart swelled the airwaves, with a sermon so deep.
So impassioned were her words to me, so devastating a plea,
Damning all the bigotry and the murderers of humanity!
Shaming all the profiteers and the promoters of religious hate,
That doom the innocent and the guilty, to their blood-drenched fate.
She poured love from her soul, a truce for true understanding,
From teardrop ripples to a flood, the good and evil branding!
Choking on her anguished words, reaching out to a million ears,
Of the butchery and intolerance, cursing us for thousands of years!
This bold and brave woman, once converted to a demonised creed,
But spoke only of God's love for us all, dawning from creation's seed!
Regardless of your skin tone or the geography of your life, be free to choose a god,
Deep goodness resounds within our hearts, yet is seldom spared the rod!
So long have the rivalries of hate, sealed the wars of attrition,
To keep the bloated money men sponsoring your ammunition!
The brainwashers, the fanatics, the pawns of the herded throng,
History burning their offspring still that the holy books teach is wrong.
The sins of our blood-letting kind still send martyrs to the stake,
Could the power of this woman's speech rebuild and help remake?
Stunned silence befell my radio then, my heart so brittle, so shaken,
For but a few minutes there, she'd healed the world and left us unforsaken!

Philip Lowe

TWIN TOWERS

We were both so tall, looking down at the roofs of many, all reaching out to the sky and sharing the view of a beautiful green park and lake in the distance.
All of us surrounded by the sea reflecting in the sunlight.
Until that awful sound of the big birds descending upon us, ripping out our hearts, allowing our souls to tumble and crush the very being of what we are.
The make-up of our body within, screaming at Death as they are engulfed in a dense fog as we topple to the floor.
Our views no longer held as we pass adjacent rooftops to lay still and crumpled at their feet.

Steve Peppin

PIDDLING POSTMAN BLUES

Since my work has changed and I'm out longer on the job
I've developed a condition where my bladder starts to throb
Because nowhere in sight is a toilet I can use
I'm suffering this plight of piddling postman blues

Monday after delivering to Mrs Jones at number three
I really found myself just bursting for a pee
I thought if I was quick I could just go behind the hedge
But it was being trimmed by her bloody husband Reg

He asked me what was up, I looked in so much pain
When I told him he suggested piddling down the drain
He said, 'If it would help I've a bucket you could use
If you think that it would ease your piddling postman blues'

At number twenty-five I was still desperate for a pee
I decided that perhaps I'd hang it out behind a tree
An irate lady shouted, 'What are you doing to my yews?'
Oh I do so hate these piddling postman blues

I'd lots of mail to get rid both second class and first
But if I did not finish soon my bladder would surely burst
To have to hold it in like that was very much a strain
And to add to my discomfort it then started to rain

When I reached ninety-seven I went to do it up the wall
I looked around and Mrs Smith was glaring from her hall
Perhaps I'll fit a pipe from my pants down to my shoes
I'll try anything to ease these piddling postman blues

By the time that I'd crossed over and got back down to number two
My predicament was worse, I was now bursting for a poo
I was really getting into such a very sorry state
Contemplating stooping down by Mrs Brown's front gate

If Mrs Brown came out she would have seen a great big log
I would have said that it was probably her next-door neighbour's dog
She would have answered that 'for dog dirt it's a very funny shade
And it's still steaming hot as if it's just been laid'

When I got back to the office I dived out of the van
I legged it up the stairs just like a mental man
After all my suffering I'd finally reached the loos
It really felt like Heaven to end those piddling postman blues.

Peter Warren

HAPPINESS, HATRED AND HOPE

A brief encounter, a short affair,
Exchange a vow, 'I'll always be there'
Gentle kisses and midnight drives
Shan't ever leave each other's lives.

Smiles and happiness for each other,
A secret wife, a real-life lover,
Looking back and looking ahead,
A promise of love until they're dead.

Quiet whispers, hiding places,
Never forget each other's faces,
Time passes, memories are made,
Words of love begin to fade.

Clouds linger above his head,
Tensions rising and words of dread.
Shocked, shivering, numb to the core
Surely this isn't worth fighting for.

Back to back, distance will grow,
Tears like a river begin to flow,
Lies and love, a lesson learned
For years they keep their backs unturned.

Uncertain future, gentle creatures
Love perfects imperfect features.
Years pass, not much to say,
She won't give in, they'll meet again one day

Hannah Oleksik

LAW

I call law not just an ass,
It is the world's only compass
Pointing its many fingers
To all the fields of Man's life.

I call law the Devil's advocate
Yet, God's only syndicate -
A bow in the hands of Devil;
An arrow in grinding grip of God.
Advocatus dei
Advocatus diaboli
The Alpha of the flame
The Omega of the Paradise.

Law is Themis
With the blindfold hovering over
Just one eye,
And freeing the other for the initiates.
Yet, sword and scales in hands
To pass a judgement fair.

I call law the master and slave,
A phenomenon with double standard
With all kinds of chameleonic brands .
Green is thy colour in spring
Yellowish-brown is it in autumn.
Father of stability
Father of instability
The certain that is uncertain
The uncertain that is certain.

Law is the inseparable Siamese twins
A wound that digs deep
Into the innocent heart of Peter
To revive Paul from his guilty sleep.
Its fact could sum up to its fiction
Its fiction could add up to its fact.

I call law the pendulum
Of all times of existence -
A determiner that will not determine,
A verb that hangs its action,
An adjective that postpones its qualification,
A hypocrite pronoun that shields identity;
Until it has conspicuously seen
Whom its object to act upon be.

Law a confusion
Law a commotion
Law a dispute conciliator
Law an arbitrator . . .
A sentence without a full stop.
A question with double question marks?

Law a hangman
Law an executioner
Law a technician
Law a politician
A creator with exclusive right to kill
A bow in the hands of the Devil
An arrow in the grip of God.

Bolaji St Ramos

THE FIRST TIME

'Twas the night before Christmas that we got the news,
In nine months we would be meeting you.
Tears of joy and smiles all round,
We couldn't believe that it was true.

We still remember the first time we saw you,
They told us you were okay, what a relief! Phew!
Eight weeks passed, we saw you again,
This time we could see your developed brain.

A long time to wait, until your estimated birth date,
But twenty weeks passed, it went so fast.
Early morning, I awoke in pain,
Waters broke, all I did was complain.

Fifteen hours passed of grunting and moaning,
Even your dad was getting fed up with my groaning!
Eventually you came into our lives,
Your dad and I couldn't believe you had finally arrived.

And still to this day, we promise we would always say,
We love you with all our hearts

In every single way.

Kerry Fisher

IAPATHETIC

I've been told that a picture speaks a thousand words,
So if I take a thousand pictures will my voice be heard?
If I take a thousand pictures do I need this verse?
See, if I recall to when I was younger I could write words first.

Before the clip of a lens, before the twit of a Tweet,
Before Facebook was tagging photos and now Facebook plans my week.
Voice detection software, where are we stopping? Nowhere.
But the warmth of the wooden pencil, and the rustle of the page.
The warmth of the wooden pencil where our imaginations were made,
The same warm wooden pencil where are our brains would play,
Not to be constricted and restricted 'write a status', 'What's happening?' 'What's on your mind today?' – Pissed off? Then Tweet away.
The truth is, you can Tweet all day because to ignore it . . . just a click away.
That's why I'm stood here in front of you because you have to hear what I want to say.
See there's power in the words and the rhythms that I sleigh,
Doing backwards gymnastics through metaphors and similes,
Trying to think up less syllabled synonyms until my brains cells are killing me.
But, what I write in a 1000 words a picture captures in one.
And who cares what I write in a thousand words? You? You? Anyone?

You see, we live in a time in which babies can use iPhones before they can speak,
A time when you're judged by your number of Tweets, not your hard work and commitment to your promising dreams.
A time in which our advances stitch our eyes blind – can't see,
A time in which, modern technology should sit down with ecology . . .
Shake his hand, smile and write the poor bloke an apology.
But that's not all the frustration off of me, I've got more to vent after this,
Now my mind is burning up blood flies like McLaren through my arteries,
Adrenaline kicks in; passion starts to squeeze my knees,
But, you sit here in silence . . . Jeez.

I don't want to change the world; I'm not looking for a new England
I mean if Billy Bragg can't do it then . . . well what chance do I have?
I mean, what chance do you have? A blunt pencil, sitting quiet.
Hoping this night will soon end and this blokes endless ranting will turn silent
And that's the modern crisis, not the credit crunch or teenagers turning violent.
The apathy in this room is the spreading disease killing everyone in silence.
I'm not trying to provoke a riot; I just hate to see people lie down, so quiet
And accept what they are given like your girlfriend faking her climax.
I'm sorry, I hate to get personal but it seems the only way to get you riled up,
Like you don't really care what happens until everything suddenly turns quite violent.
You're quite happy to be the English man, join the queue, accept and wait.
But when you get to the front, and they've ran out. You're always first to complain.
What's wrong with a little debate? Express your views and how you feel,

After all we live in a democratic society – that's what you are encouraged to do, right?

Oh wait, I mean, the voting station is at least ten minutes away and it's getting kinda dark.
And in your area a no vote is a vote for BNP, which kinda seems a good laugh.
Or maybe the Monster Raving Loony Party will finally win so rather than getting the bus to college you could ride a pogo stick in.
See, I don't want to change the world; I'm not looking for a new England.
I'll just continue to be played by the system and accept some Eton schoolboy's wisdom.
Because, apathy is the silent killer and I'll be happy doing nothing.
But when the killer grabs me, that's when I'll go down shouting.

George Martindale

DREAMING

Colours,
red, blue, green,
purple and pink –
All mixing and merging
Into the most beautiful picture
you have ever seen,
and yet,
cannot be described.

You can feel the sun
on your face –
So real, it almost is.

The air lifts you off the ground
and you are flying
Through trees and
above seas,
Until you glide to a stop,
back in bed.

Rhiana Henderson

YOU ARE THE FOE OF LOVE

I wanted to bring you to,
The vast beach of my hope.
Your rejection always constant,
Taking me where I could not cope.

You took me to the doldrums,
Filled my hope with pain,
The sea of all my tears,
Washed away every sandy grain.

The beach of my hope is empty,
Lost to the water of your well.
Hidden you always wanted me.
Every day said more, of me you repel.

You squashed all of my dreams,
You squandered our potential path.
With such a destructive attitude,
That suggested nothing but hateful wrath.

You made love an enemy,
An opponent to deal with danger.
For me who loved you oh so much,
You treated indifferently, as a stranger.

I could not catch your gaze,
Each glance held much disgust,
After giving away my heart to you,
I felt manipulated with such distrust.

For you treated me like a player,
Within a game of poker,
When I raised my heart in too,
You thought, *fool, I intend to choke ya.*

You took me to the cleaners,
Though you never showed your hand,
For where loves dwells you kept away,
Never visiting such a land.

The one time you flew over.
You dropped a more deadly Hiroshima.
The effects of which still reverberate,
Claiming that you'd never seen her.

The woman who never believed in love,
Or ever gave it sufficient a chance,
'What does my selfish soul want,
With something as giving as romance?'

Poked me with great criticism
Pepper sprayed my sight,
You starved me of all possible care,
Then toyed with me 'til I bite.

You took me from temperate home,
To a place of resenting depression.
You cooked my bones in naked flames,
For I was not a person, but a possession.

I could take the deadening burns,
For wishing you'd one day stop,
In the potential happiness of our lives,
You'd let us make it to the top.

But when you'd finished all your fun,
Bored of terrorizing my life,
You ousted out your winnings,
Making sure you'd never be my wife.

You put a dagger in my heart,
I'd prefer a bullet in the head.
For I have no idea where to start,
Removing such pain and dread.

It is my own fault,
For daring to be so bold.
For love could never warm you up,
Towards me . . . you're always cold.

Robbie Potter

IN LOVE'S KIND LAND

In Love's kind land,
we make our stand
with kisses of rebel.
Our hearts ablaze,
when Love's sweet gaze
come to see them fell.
No partings made,
when hand to spade
and fall to the deep abyss.
In Love's kind land
we made our stand,
how small was one last kiss

Phoebe Elizabeth Luckham

A WISH COME TRUE

Picture a little girl, sleeping soundly in her bed
Breathing oh so softly, a pillow underneath her head
Something then awoke, this little girl called Mary
Upon the pillow next to her, sat a pretty fairy
'Who are you?' Mary asked, 'and why are you here?'
The fairy pulled a grumpy face, 'Now you listen dear
I don't do small talk, so don't you bother me
Who and the why for, they just don't matter see
It seems you did a kindness, for the lady down the road'
'She grumpily turned purple, looked like she may explode'
'Well now,' she continued, 'this is what I have to do
Grant one special wish, one especially for you
But hurry girl, make it now, for I have a lot to do
Better places I should be, not stuck in here with you
And don't go being greedy, no fame, no wealth, or cash
Make a wish like that my girl, and I'll turn you to ash'
Well one sleepy little girl, she thinks really hard
While the fairy tuts and groans, staring no regard
'Oh,' the little girl said, 'I know what I'll wish
I want to hear the animals, the birds, the bugs, the fish
I want to understand them and hear what they say
I will listen for hours, each and every day'
'At last you really took your time,' angry fairy said
She waved her magic wand, above her little head
Then with a final scowl, the grumpy fairy disappeared
The little girl went back to sleep, thinking that was weird
In the morning she awoke, to a voice in her left ear
It was Fluffy her pet cat, talking and she could hear
'Look at this dozy girl,' the cat so loudly said
'It is well past sunrise and she is still in bed
I have to let her stroke me, give her my big eyes
Pretend to love these humans, I secretly despise'
Mary could not believe it, heard everything she said
The cat purred and nuzzled her, Mary pushed it off the bed
'Are you OK sweetie?' her mummy asked, and felt her brow
But Mary couldn't hear her, over the fish making a row
All the fish were babbling, struggling to agree
Which was the best way, to the Pacific Sea
They didn't seem to realise, that they were in a tank
Round and around they swam, seemed silly to be frank
Mary ran into the garden, through a spider's web
The spider he was furious, called the girl a pleb
Her neighbour was upon her horse, her neighbour is called Pat
The horse whinnied 'Get her off of me, she is so very fat'

This is how the day went, with every animal she found
Every bird up in the sky, each critter on the ground
Not one was happy, they moaned all the day
Not what Mary hoped for, none wanted to play
She went to bed early, fed up with her wish
Put her pillow over her head, to drown out the fish
Then with a puff of smoke, the fairy she was back
Carrying her fairy dust, in a little sack
'Well child,' she said to Mary, 'it's now that you must choose
Will you keep your wish forever, or the power will you lose'
'Take it away,' Mary said, 'I can't stand no more
The animals won't shut up, my ears they are sore'
The fairy laughed a cackle, said some magic words
The fish they fell silent, as did the moaning birds
'Did you learn anything, from the gift you got today?'
Mary thought real hard, she had a few things to say
'Sometimes its better not to know, things that you should not
Some things are better kept unsaid and other things forgot
But I also know what makes animals sad, horses down to ants
They have a lot of issues, they have a lot of rants'
The fairy had a giggle, 'Mary tell me what you mean
Whatever could upset an ant, what could they find obscene?'
'I will tell you,' Mary said, 'what upsets worse than carbuncles
It's the fact we call them ants, when half of them are uncles!'

Gary Wickson

THE LITTLE CREATURES

Oh! I didn't mind that much,
When one of the little creatures, ran down my hand.
I found it very adorable,
And left it on a leaf.
But, I must admit it,
I was a little surprised,
When the first one was followed by a second of its own kind.
But, all the same this one too seemed adorable,
And I left it on a leaf.
But imagine my surprise when I saw that,
The second was being followed by a third, a fourth and a fifth of its own kind.
And even before I knew it my entire arm was covered with ants,
It was only then that I realised that I had stepped into an ant hole!

Elsa Mariam Ninan

IN LOVING MEMORY OF MY AUNTIE LORRAINE, GRANDAD ERIC AND MY NANNA MARGARET

Three truly special members of my family
Have sadly passed

They mean so much to me
they have special memories
that are precious and cherishing
they belong in my heart

I believe that they are right with me
when I wish upon a star

Every night, before the light goes out
I pray to the stars that I believe in
I would pray to them when I write poetry

After praying to the stars that I wish upon
at night and day
The faces of my three family members
They glow from the sky at night

They smile down at me
They show that they are proud
They tell me how much I am loved

After my three stars have answered my prayers
I feel proud with happy tears

I am very spiritual
In my very own way
With love and I am kind-hearted

I am a king in my own way and style
with special achievements

Tom Brealey

THE FINGERPOST

We started where four roads met.
No tales to tell nor to regret.
And stood in the shadow of names long dead;
Ours not yet worthy to be read.

As lads we traipsed these four old roads,
And the lanes that fed their flow,
And kicked the heads from flowers
For their impudence to grow.

But then we were giants and they were not;
They blurred the borders of our tracks.
They were pink and purple smudges
On the stencilled lines of black.

Yet Hydra's stumps we left unburned
And year on year the heads returned
And glad we became to see them back
To line the borders of our tracks.

Cos though we are still yet to choose
Which finger to obey,
Those heads no longer blur our lines -
No lines to blur in worlds of grey -
But puncture skies of shapeless fog,
Like beacons in the mist,
And though our paths remain unclear,
We know that they exist.

Adam Leese

THE CITY AT NIGHT

Now the nightclub's empty
Streets, littered with rubbish
Detritus, that escaped the bin
Neons, stutter brokenly, flashing
Their unwanted, welcome message.

Silence now broken, by *odd* shouts
As late-goers, drift homeward
Lamps, move in wind, miscast shadows
Letters darkly gesture, in yellow paint
'No parking', either needed, or wanted.

Ozone, filters back exhaust gas
While, in subway (much beloved)
Of civic planners, lurid graffiti
Beckons in, innuendo and slander
Saving Facebook, harassment in court.

Silhouetted, denizens disrobe, as
One-by-one, window lights extinguish
Cats whine and patrol, restless
Walls, topped with broken glass
The city, hums into kilowatt slumber . . .

A G McRobb

WHAT'S IN A NAME? (THAT WHICH WE CALL A ROSE)

Looking back on my given name.

It came as a great relief
That my parents called me Keith,
To be truthful it could have been a curse
A nightmare or something worse.

Something that really could have filled me with shame.

A title that could have been shortened like Michael.

That would really have been taking the Mick
Like Richard being shortened to Dick,
Barry going down to Baz
And Gary going down to Gaz.

A name is something that shouldn't be recycled.

Your name should be forever.

Sacred to you for all time
The blueprint that makes up your design,
A characteristic that is part of you
A kind of moral fibre glue.

That holds your very core together.

But then the petals fell off my rose.

When I found out I had not been baptized
It was then that I realised,
If God doesn't know my name
Then how can I claim

To be who I am, I suppose?

Keith Tissington

THE MAN WITH NO FRIENDS

I am an outcast, a freak they say,
But I can't help it, I was born this way.
People look and point when I walk down the street,
Women, children and even pensioners spit at my feet.
Even my family will not accept me
When I was four months they put me up on ebay and they didn't get a penny.
They said they weren't surprised that I didn't sell,
Because they said a thing like me, should belong in Hell.
I knew I would always be alone, and that was a fact
Because I was not only born ginger but I was born black.
It would be okay if I was just black because I would have a crew,
I would listen to hip-hop and wear Converse shoes.
It would be okay if I was ginger and have a gang
I would wear burgundy hats and make up slang.
I tried to shave my head but it would always grow back,
I even thought to do a Michael Jackson with my skin but I felt I would look like a twat.
I would try and talk to people and they would call me a prick,
And smile at little children but they would literally be sick.
So you could understand how I haven't lost my virginity,
I couldn't even buy it off a prostitute when I was at university.
So I am still searching for the one
A ginger big mama would be lots of fun.
I would not care about looks or personality
Only if she could accept me into society.
You can have AIDS or HIV
I am a ginger black man, it wouldn't make a difference to me.
I'm just looking for somebody to love
I will let you sit below my chin or just above.
I tried dating sites, would work for a while,
Then they would see my photo and run a mile.
But I can have a chuckle and laugh about this all now,
Even laugh at the time people tried to crucify me in the centre of town.
Because I have found somebody and it feels so good
When I'm with her I can even take down my hood,
And the thing I love most about my dear Caroline,
Is the fact that she is severely blind.

Samuel Riseley

SHOES

I am not a shopper of shoes
Are you? Which ones would you choose?
I remember at school getting the slipper.
Naughty? I don't recall I was a nipper.

I never really liked my shoes for school.
Not that I purposely broke the rules
They were big and black with a huge rubber heel
Not a shoe that allows a girl to be gentile

After school, I wore heels as I worked the bar.
'Ooh a good pair of legs 'n' heels could slow a speeding car'
Hmm, some more than others notice the shoes
And share their fantasy, ha, like they get to choose!

Flats and trainers. Heels for the bar.
Oh but they don't fair well when driving a car.
Then I venture out and join a band
And at the big reveal we show our hand (feet)

The début gig went down a treat.
Never! No. Listening or watching our feet?
Elated with the first set going down a storm
Then through the crowd, a bloke far from the norm

He spoke to Bev and whispered in her ear
Said how pleased he was we'd played here
Pleasantries done and she made a move
Oh no lady, he was in the groove

For then he dealt a killer line
'I love your shoes, sexy, my mum wore those FM shoes all the time'

Donna Giblin

FRIDAY NIGHT BLUES

Shaky ebony fingers
linger on pearl keys,
as the cream of music
pounds the heartbreaking blues
and frenzied cuties take
up forlorn men and cling them
to their bosoms

And the music eases their souls

As dreams are put on hold,
horns blast out through
darkened nights,
carried by laughing couples
clinging onto cigarettes and beer

as the melody lingers still

stocky fingers fly over moody tunes
and crazy dancers take to
the floor, shrieking at the
seducing rhythm of weary blues
and Monday morn comes

a distant memory

as wild feet move like
a soul possessed by
hopeless grooves and excited eyes,
all dreams pinned on

the blues man

with his anaesthetic jingle
and sorrowful megrims of wisdom

Leah-Marie Mills

NIGHT AND KNIVES

It was a cold autumn night
And all was quiet
The sky was deep cobalt
Streaked with violet
A veil of mist
Drifted through the streets
Singing sweet words
To the people it meets
And though all the strangers
Slowly walk by
Alone in an alleyway
A little boy lay
Cold and soundless
He lay there huddled
His body was numb
His mind was muddled
The blood that he laid in
Wouldn't bring to a halt
He did nothing wrong
It wasn't his fault
Beside him lay the blade
That had done the deed
The night felt sympathy
As he would continue to bleed
It is times like these
That causes so much strife
Killed in the night by
Power of the knife
And this is why
Our kids we must defend
And together we can put
This madness to an end

Emma Boddy

TROUBLE EXPLODED

and I realised,
it is a dream
and I don't want to wake up.
As was to be expected,
even if there was a hand,
it was the hand of God,
but I thought
I did it with the hand of reason, with the mind's eye.
That is why I always make the sign of the cross.
A sign which delves through me, into the unknown.
When I am asleep
The spirits whisper madly inside my head,
they say
give me a place to stand, and I will move the Earth,
but I need a lever and a fulcrum,
but I want to lift it with my hands,
but now I have erased this line, and now I think.

There is no great genius without some touch of madness.
I realised this when
I became insane, with long intervals of horrible sanity.
Now
I believe it is the biggest thing in the human race,
and the most constant.
Constantly changing and developing and altering and shaping.
How do you take away from a man his madness
without also taking away his identity?
Madness brings stronger identity.

For me life is continuously being hungry.
Sleep, breathe and love
are such food that give life perspective.
The meaning of life
is not simply to exist,
to survive, but to move ahead, to go up, to achieve, to conquer.
I really don't think money matters.
Money doesn't make you happy.
Strength is always more important than money.
Strength does not come from winning.
Your struggles develop your strengths.
For when I am weak,
Then I am strong.
Don't try, do or don't do.
When you go through hardships
and decide not to surrender,

that is strength.
Physical strength comes
from the best activities for your health,
pumping and humping.
People don't know much until hardship.
What I have learned is that we are always
stronger than we know
and
that which does not kill me makes me stronger,

but
my decision is taken.
Either complete freedom or holocaust.
I intellectualised, no I thought,
a trail of orange peels
would lead me to it -
'If',
The word which makes people shudder.
When I saw the breadth of my domain
I wept
for there were no more worlds to conquer . . .
. . . If only . . .
'If'.
. . . If only
my reward was my own being.
Even still,
they tried to crush me and failed.

Andreas Koutsoudis

MISS MOORE

This one's for you, Miss Moore!

Miss Moore - student teacher – student teacher of the sciences
Miss Moore – with all your gifts and surprises of concealed female splendour.
Miss Moore - having difficulty with some of the teen male component in your class,
Especially two of them.
Miss Moore - questioning yourself where you were going wrong with us,
Kev and I questioning ourselves - where we were going wrong with you!

But you did the right thing, Miss Moore, sending us to detention day after day
Giving us time to spend more time with you!
You made us grin with such a privilege, hot teacher!
And while there, Miss Moore

You would come closer to the desk Kev and I shared
And repeat carefully in your sweetest voice, 'What's the matter, boys?'

What's the matter?
We could only laugh in response, Miss Moore,
while your supervisor watched you from the back of the class
But deep inside, I groaned when you said that, Miss Moore,
If only you knew what was going on with us
But teen boys weren't on your diet,
we could see that.
We were happy to take our positions a few hundred thousand rungs down the hormonal ladder:

waiting, giggling, and hoping - the way dumb teen boys hope

Dreaming for you to teach us:
the exquisiteness of the sciences,
the neatness and beauty of biology,
The flow of chemistry
and the eternal mysteries of diverse copulation.

Miss Moore, with your stimulation,
I almost refrained from complete high school apathy
As expected in precise school tradition
to make a half-hearted attempt to compete
to be your most devoted and avid pupil
My tight pants hitting the A grade!

But yes, Miss Moore, you guessed it!
Kev and I were sooo in need of discipline.

Discipline and PVC,
Bondage, leather and harsh words.

We were in need of education Miss Moore – tutelage just with you
Our bodies demanded it.

Education within the sweet privacy of your uncomfortable, smelly lab.
But, Miss Moore, I guess you never really figured it all out with us,
And I do hope you passed your later student teacher days with less confusion than when you were with us,
So that you could go on and give other classrooms of young males
The fullest and most frustrating of lessons.

But Kev and I – well, we were lucky, Miss Moore,

Our lunchtimes
Did not go to waste
with you –

Gorgeous student teacher!

Brad Evans

LOST GENERATION

A boy lays in the gutter
a needle by his side
a life so short, a last resort
he even lost his pride
he lived without a future
then died without a life
he will never know the happiness
of children and a wife
they say it will not harm you
they say you will feel no pain
for they know once you try it
that you will be back again
for a pusher makes a million
he makes it out of sorrow
another trip, another hit
another death tomorrow

John Frankie Connor

HAPPINESS

You think that you know them
Right to the ground
Inside out
Round and round
You've been with them for over a year
Without shedding a single tear

Then they make a small remark
Different form what you'd expect
Your world then comes tumbling down
Like water on rocks

You can't take any chances
And you can't show them you care
Because then, all of your dreams
Will just meet blocks

You just have to imagine
What life could be with someone else
Without feeling the hurt or pain
That you would with them

You can try to find someone else
Until you give up
You could find happiness by having fun
With a new special someone

Happiness is being yourself
Not being someone identical
Happiness is living the dream
And not being a book on a shelf

Alice Marshall

DO SWANS EAT KOI?

Did you too see it, drifting,
all night, on the black river?
Did you see it in the morning?
rising into the silvery air -
An armful of white blossoms,
A perfect commotion
Of silk and linen as it leaned
Into the bondage of its wings;
A snow bank, a drift of white lilies,
Biting the air with its black beak.
Did you hear it, fluting and whistling
A shrill dark music?
Like the rain pelting the trees -
Like a waterfall
Knifing down the black ledges.
And did you see it, finally,
Just under the clouds?
A white cross streaming across the sky,
Its feet
Like black leaves, its wings
Like the stretching light of the river.
And did you feel it,
In your heart,
How it pertained to everything?
And have you too finally
Realised what beauty is for?
And has it changed your life?

Elizabeth Davies

GOOD FRIENDS THAT WILL NEVER SAY GOODBYE

I can never say goodbye to someone so dear
as it would make me cry, as the tears
flow from my eyes.

I will always keep friends like you
close and near to me, as
I couldn't bear to be apart
as you have really touched my
life and my heart.

I think of you each day, missing you
more than words can say.
I cannot wait to see you again
where we can have a good laugh
and a giggle and smile the whole
day through, happy times
make for happy memories
shared with friends so dear
like you.

Leanne Perks

THE CATS

Jiji and Yoyo,
Black and white.
They should be called
Salt and Pepper.
No, said Capucine,
No, emphasize Candice.
Jiji walks, elegantly as a catwalk.
Yoyo clumsy hits and drops objects.
C'est fou ce chat, says Valérie.
Being haunted by a big white ghost dog
Has moments of madness.
Runs, jumps, screams, meows,
So funny my cute pie, says Salomé.

Clovis Willy

SORRY

I'm sorry Mom, I can hear you cry
Death was recruiting, I decided to apply
Truly sorry, for the pain inflicted
Depression was my drug, to which I was addicted

We fought and argued, laughed and cried
You were always there, right by my side.
I thought about you, as I took my life
Thought about the good times as I reached for the knife

You're not at fault, please don't accept blame
No desire to live, so I smothered the flame
Not a friend in the world, why would I stay?
Persistently bullied, resolve faded away.

December 31st, the day that Death replied
I passed the interview, so glad I applied
I took the pills, took Dad's beer
Life was too hectic, I simply lived in fear

Mom, you found me, sprawled on the floor
A bloody mess, breathing no more
'Oh God, baby, please don't leave.'
You held me tight; it was New Year's Eve.

I'm sorry Mom; I have ruined your life
That grisly episode, those pills, that knife,
I tried to fight, but misery took hold
Your only child's dead, barely 14 years old.

John Glynn

A GIRL WHO FULFILLED HER DREAM

There once lived a girl rich, beautiful and lovely,
Being the only child she was dealt preciously.
She lived her life merrily and to the zenith,
Every day soaring higher with the world left beneath,
Like others she too was gifted which wasn't a mystery,
In twisting words and carving out of them some great poetry,
She once heard that great poetry comes from a heart which is broken, painful and dejected,
It's only then true emotions and feelings to the dead words are imparted,
She realised her passion and kept writing,
A flame to be a poet in her kept igniting,
But alas life had something else for her in store,
She was burdened with the responsibilities her family upon her had bestowed,
To be the heir of her family's immense fortune,
She was snatched away from her dream of writing poems,
Forced to keep away from the so-called useless hobby of writing,
She felt reckless for her heart was slowly breaking,
She had with her a prosperous future and everything,
But something deep down was indeed greatly missing,
Her delicate shoulders couldn't uphold the burden,
Also not being able to give up her dream she passed into depression,
Slowly her body and soul gave way,
When she stopped breathing one day,
Amazingly some new poetry work was found within her belongings,
The world cried in vain upon realising,
That they silenced not only her words,
But also did they broke her heart,
Her poetry was later published as a tribute,
The work was immensely applauded and received with gratitude,
For years and years she wasn't forgotten, for her writing gathered unmatchable fame,
Though she was silenced but she left behind carved in history - Her poetry, her name . . .

Syeda Amna

LAMBS

Those dark villages of childhood
And dimly-lit memories
Dusty springs and coils
Waiting for a little hand to
Reach out and be
Changed.

And the dirty forest in which
Roamed monsters
Leeches of innocence
Pests of Good.

The sound of silence
After a crack
A slap
A shot
Entreating to the shadowy circles around
A 'grown-up's' heart.

It is said
The river that flows within you
It's all tears really.

Starving people made of hunger
Of a different kind.

Hanna Wulkan

AMAZING GRACE

This is the tale of amazing Grace,
And her jaunts on the wild trapeze.
Her sparkly tights caused pulses to race,
(You should see what she did with her knees.)

Grace was the star of Bernardo's Big Top,
Her feats were simply astounding.
She caused the spectators' breathing to stop,
Their applause was loud and resounding.

Her refusal to use a strong safety net,
Put frowns on worried white faces.
But she was a show-off and said, 'Oh don't fret,
just enjoy my amazing graces.'

Her fellow performers got so very sick,
Of Grace's outrageous loud swanking.
They said, 'What we'll do with this pesky young chick,
Is to give her a bloody sound spanking.'

'I'll do it, I'll do it!' squeaked Colin the Clown,
His eyes were like saucers and popping.
'It'll hurt even more if I rip those tights down,
And give her a really hard whopping.'

'That's just so not fair,' whined Peter (fire-eater),
'We should all be allowed one smack each,'
'This is not for enjoying for God's sake Peter!
It's a lesson we just need to teach.'

Deciding to be a little more daring,
Our Gracie attempted new tricks.
Hung on by big toe without really caring,
Performed one of her super high kicks.

It was one kick too far and she crashed to the ground,
Every bone in her body had shattered.
Her 'friends' gasped and cried and then bustled around,
(Pretending that she'd really mattered.)

There was no kiss of life Grace had simply deceased
Though Colin insisted he'd try.
Pete said, 'For God's sake man, don't be such a beast,'
(As his thumb caressed Grace's cold thigh).

Rigor mortis set in, she began to go stiff,
Eyes open, no sign of a blink.
Death's gases emitted a final sad whiff
Grace grinned then gave Peter a wink.

Shirley McIntyre

IF ONLY THERE WAS 'SKYPE' IN HEAVEN

If only there was 'Skype' in Heaven, if only for a day,
I would call and speak to you for hours,
Big talk, and small talk and just,
About the simple little things that sisters have to say.

We would talk about the weather and what each season has to bring,
Especially about the flowers that I hope will bloom again this spring.
I think I might plant some petunias, and perhaps some roses too
That's if I get the time of course, I still have plenty of other little jobs to do.
'You know how it is!'

Oh, and what about earlier this year, when the first snow fell,
My God, it was awful, way too cold for me and far too deep
But it didn't stop our little kids from snowballing and bob-sleighing in the street,
Bless them! They were having so much fun their little faces told it all!
They didn't even notice their freezing hands and feet – 'or so they said'
Don't know who they are trying to fool! – Do you?
'Just hope they don't get chilblains'

Here's a turn up for the book! My friend has just divorced the other half
She's even bought new clothes and shoes,
And dyed her hair a lovely shade of chestnut-brown
Nudge, nudge, wink, wink, I think there could be someone new in town!
'Not that I'm, being nosey, but watch this space – I'll keep you posted'

And what with all this technology moving faster than the speed of light,
Do you think they will put in a 'Skype link' to Heaven? – 'Fingers crossed'
Who knows, they just might.
But this is only 'let's pretend' and my imaginations running riot.
'Wishful Thinking on my part'

But then, you will never be forgotten, not if I have my way,
For you are locked within my heart
And never far away
'If only there was Skype in Heaven'
We could chat, chat, chat all day.

Diana J Stouchbury

SCENIC FANATIC

His fist connected,
The most gentle of kisses,
Memories of Makarovs,
And begging forgiveness.

Sat by the window
In our room,
Threading the needle,
I've been stitching his wounds.

The flippant pedant,
Fripperies and vagrancy,
That's a no, and a no.
When I'm the child bride
In the next life
On the death row.

A pedagogue
Was Eros
Was my God/God's
Grave dust.

All decent extremists,
And indecent bulimics,
Spiel and polemics,
Scenic fanatic.

The most aesthetic of addicts,
(This girl's gone quite rabid)
I'm the wife in the attic,
(And it's all rather tragic)

The glass half full
Emptied by the clumsy
Psychopath. Would you teach me
How to shoot? I've been
Schooled by the jackboot.

Aleksandra

UNTITLED

I'm going to die!
(And so am I!)
Write me in this picture
Draw me in this song
Sing me along, as giggling, I sigh
Catch me this video
Play it so high!
Nothing is wrong –
But I'm going to die!

Snap me in knickers
Trap me in glue
Sell me a streetboy –
Hold me to you!
Make me your story
Wrap me in lies
No need for emoting –
But I'm going to die!

Call me a leftie –
Remove my right eye
Know how I've loved you
Bye-bye . . .
Going to die . . .
So am I . . .

Jon Elkon

LORD WALTER'S BUSH

'But why do you go?' said my Lady, elegantly sat under the yew,
As I hide behind this budding bush, wondering what I should do.

Who is that I behold? My good friend Franklin I'm sure.
With my lady he is speaking, or does he insinuate more?

Just my luck to be passing, and stumble upon such a thing,
Will my wife stay loyal and true? How much faith is there in that ring?

'I value your husband Lord Walter,' I hear from behind this damn bush,
What is my wife really saying, my buttons she is starting to push.

Can I trust this dear woman my wife, with this lifelong friend of mine?
Has she made a promise to another? As well as the one made to thine.

Why am I being so silly? Of course I have full trust in my wife,
When a vow is made at the altar, it is a vow made for eternal life.

Why does he speak of my daughter? What things to hear on my stroll,
My sweet little angel Dora, what a perfectly crafted doll.

'Although you should please me and stay,' the words leave her lips with such ease,
This is not lady-like behaviour, I be the only man she should please.

My back aches as I crouch down, if only I could move discreetly,
I feel the need to speak with my wife; I want my mind eased completely.

A raised voice I hear as I hover, what can be going on now?
I don't want my wife to discover me, to think I am spying somehow.

Why does Franklin speak of my wife, questioning how she is fair?
Her fairness is very apparent, in her truth, her love and her care.

Ugly and hateful he swears, how dare he so strongly insult.
Is now the time to reveal myself, will that move provide any result?

What can I hear over there? My love she so boldly sounds,
She laughs out so loud in scorn, her tinkling giggles resound.

'Why Sir I am pure and a wife,' she says, defending her honour with strength,
Why did I doubt her at all? My apologies she deserves at great length.

A fallen woman she is not, but what does that make Franklin to me?
A friend, a foe, an enemy, what is he trying to be?

'I love my Walter profoundly,' those words touch my heart straight away,
I want to hold her this instant, in love a place we shall stay.

I feel I should try to move now, my time here has come to an end,
My wife proved so strong and so glorious, no need for me to defend.

Franklin has left the garden, how shameful he has been,
If I'd taken his word for this event, a disgrace it would have been seen.

What would have been spoken of her, if I had not witnessed the truth,
Considered a disloyal woman? Could she have been the next Ruth?

She turns so I make an attempt, quickly I try to flee,
'Daddy, Daddy,' cries sweet Dora, I try to turn her from me.

'Your mother Dora, go there,' she must be quiet I fear,
My wife she should never know, behind this bush I was here.

Rising up to make the move, away from this secretive place,
Turning to walk towards my own home, I'm met with my wife's pure face.

Laura McGregor

ALWAYS IN MY HEART

As I sit here thinking,
Shoulders oh so heavy,
I feel a warmth embrace me,
Your arms to hold me steady.

The days seem sometimes endless,
Now that you're not near,
I close my eyes and think of you,
As you wipe away my tears.

I talk to you for hours,
And people think I'm mad,
But I smile as I remember,
Conversations we have had.

And even when I'm sleeping,
I know that you are there,
Ready to hold and comfort me,
When life seems so unfair.

Chantay Speed

I'M ANGRY, WHY AREN'T YOU?

Asking me, so surreptitiously
why I'm ranting and raving
crazy and scathing?
Refusing to just let it go
accept the status quo.
You tell me that 'this, *is* equality
feminism its over and done.
and guess what, we won.'

But I'm hurt . . .
by your look of disgust
as it works its way up
The way that you, tut and strut.
Cosmo girl on some glorious mission
my ultimate submission
to these, paper-thin superstars
ribs poking through skin
and singing their
hymns of redemption.

Goddesses
of the aesthetics and cosmetics
training up their spawns
to wage a war
against my feminine form.
appointing you with the authority
to place your hands upon your hips
and pronounce your verdict.
That I'm a disgrace
to the female race
with these prickly hairs upon my face
and that's not to mention
my spare tired waist.

You tell me that . . .
'it's just low self-esteem
which has you wearing
these baggy jeans, but don't worry
'cause it's nothing
a little bit of lipstick won't fix.'

As you
pluck, prune and squeeze me
into your pet project beauty queen.

I'm falling apart
at these seams.

Tired of playing, your intelligent
but slightly frumpy sidekick.
Tired of waiting at the bar
for him to pick.
Tired of pimping myself out
putting on a sexy show
for him and his mates
as they think about date rape.
While I gyrate
on the dance floor
to Britney and to Pink
pretending that
I'm still seventeen
some coy teenage wet dream.

Angry that I was naive
enough to believe
that I was the most
beautiful women
he'd ever seen.
Angry that I let him
interrupt me mid flow
that I tittered at his sexist jokes.
That I thought it was romantic
When he said
'You've pulled, go get your coat'

That I limped back to his
barefooted and blistered
for a drunken fumble
beneath his dirty sheets.
That I waited, for over a week
curled up by telephone
cradling this guilt
between my thighs.

Angry that I, was nothing
but 'a quick fuck'.
That he, he gets to be the stud
while I'm just his dirty little slut.
A collection of disembodied parts
pussy, tits and arse
a conquest, a victim, a plaything
an empty vessel for him
to stick himself in.

So tired of being defined
by this body
and not my mind.

Angry and betrayed
by the thought
that it's been and done
over and won
and that we have been rescued
by these rights to consume.

Branded whores
begging for more.
Selling ourselves off
and buying ourselves back in bits.

So yes, I guess
I'm angry and I'm rude
and I don't wear what I should
I sweat rather than glow
and I'm finally, learning
how to say . . . *no!*

I won't roll over and shut up
I won't slow down
'cause you can't keep up.

I wont stifle back
my feminine rage
at this, a pornified age.

My question is
I'm angry, why aren't you?

Nicola Watt

DEATH BY TRAY

It all went wrong, it's clear to me
When trying to impress on bended knee

With hindsight, you're right
It was rather strange
But I was nervous and exposed on an open range

My inner monologue then lost the plot
And groped at straws to fix this strop

A comedic gem, Eddie Izzard's 'Death by Tray'
Vader queuing at the Death Star Café
An argument flares over a catering gaff
Believe me
It's funny!
How could anyone not laugh?

A smorgasbord of silence, tumbleweeds roll by
My version of the cross dresser - truly dies
Tilting at windmills, try to be as smooth as Oil of Olay
No good,
To you I'm as mad as Don Quixote

We discussed the last time we had both cried
My immediate response
'United, 99, the European Cup winning side'
Compared with her tearful choice of Atonement
I lost my chance of being her Heathcliff moment

Randomly, I blather on about the slang of the Cockneys
Thinking this might make her weak at the 'chips and peas'
No response is forthcoming; I begin to sense her rancour
She thinks therefore I am
A total 'Kuwaiti Tanker'

We rise and exchange the compulsory air kisses
She smiles, but her body language hisses
The words of Marx
Groucho not Karl
'I've had a wonderful time, but this wasn't it'

Peretz Tabor

FIFTEEN MINUTES OF FAME

She'd come forward, of course, when they asked for witnesses.
It's wicked what can happen to kiddies these days.
Just not safe anywhere.
Anyway, she'd told the police she'd seen this man
In a blue anorak,
With a little girl holding his hand
Walking towards the old quarry.
Course, the police were all over the quarry like a rash,
Two or three big vans and all taped off.

She'd been on the 6 o'clock news,
Standing right outside her house.
and later on the ten o'clock,
Only that was only on the local,
The weekly came round and interviewed her,
Only that didn't come out while Thursday.

And by that time they'd found her body
In the park
Right the other side of the town.

Poor little soul.

Gillian Peall

COMPLEXITIES

I've seen the roof of the top of the Earth
Seen volcanoes give lands new birth
Swam the deepest of the ocean floor
Opened Heaven's door
Felt the rains pour
Surprises held in store
Witnessed the birth of a child
Felt the wilderness in the wild
Held the warm sun on my face
Been welcomed to a friendly place
Explored the realms of space
Watched an angel fall from grace
Saw battles fought and won
Constructed wonders, built and done
Technology in its wonderous breath
Saw relatives at their loss, grieve
Tricks pulled from a sleeve
None believers, believe
Knowledge in its infinite wisdom sought
Thinkers pondered deep in thought
Writers create the word
Music and images, seen and heard
All these things witnessed and seen
The actions of a human being
The gentle flight of the dove
But who can understand the complexities of love?

Terry J Powell

MOTIONLESS

Without any distinct emotion
But still no trace of confusion
Yet confused
Seems that's all life is to a life without direction

Subjected to the beliefs of the world that surrounds us
Suppressed by the stigma of the religious beliefs that are fenced around us
The notion of what might be is put down by what has already been
The way we want to live is being put down by what 'their' eyes have seen
Motionless
The mindset with no approval and yet seeking non
The boundaries we place around ourselves
Yet there is no set procession of how things must be
'Be you,' they say,
'But just don't do this or that'
Boundaries . . .
so we stay . . . motionless!

A complex that's become a hereditary disease,
Skinning the body of life of dreams and ambitions
Injected by inbalming fluid of limitations
That in turn infects the brain and spreads the virus to our hands and feet
Our eyes wide open but still refusing to see further than today
So we remain motionless
All we are seems to be hopeless

Yes
We say yes to the things we hear
Yet do we consider more than what we've heard
Or seemingly forget that there is more to life than the little box we are sitting in
There's more to us that what we perceive
There's more we can accomplish if we can only believe
Believe in ourselves and we can climb high mountains
Cross valleys and find the treasure that our destiny contains

So many people cripple themselves
Live like vagabonds and place ambitions on the shelves
And so many live life so careless
And the results then, they become motionless
But all is said and done and we must move on
Searching for a solution within to move forward from here-on

The inspiration leaving the system and thoughts flowing in
So from this point on, this is the last,
For now it is just motionless

Charity Everjoy Tafirenyika

GREETINGS FROM THE ICONOCLAST ISLES

Forgive us, we won't mean to give offence,
if we accept things with a pinch of salt.
Our national fault, the British just must take the piss.
Don't misread this; those times of innocence
when we were pompous, white and right,
with the pink map, the sun that never set, they're gone.
Shove them where the sun has never shone.
Only uniforms remain, brash monumental stone,
marble fig leaves, guilt and stolen art.
Those years we were supposed to rule the waves
taught us that figureheads have feet of clay,
so that today, we couldn't give a farthing's worth of fart.

Don't hold with dogma, demagogues
who claim veracity. We trust to none, indeed
most princes turn out frogs. Uncertainty's our creed.
Embarrassed at successes past and gone,
are proud to be best losers on the Earth.
Our men and women err in equal worth.
We love our neighbours for their faults and warmth of heart
and one another for the same, take in good part:
cockney rhyming bankers, tabloid sleaze,
paparazzi, politicians, the police.

Albion boasts no bloodstock, rag-bag land
of races, creeds. We warm to hear them speak:
a Chinese Scouser, Geordie Sikh,
Somali Brummy, cut glass Oxford Caribbean.
We're all of these and more, diverse, the same,
and everyone's a target for a laugh,
with some to love, and some to love to hate:
the Beeb, the Queen, hoodies, gay and straight,
those with opinions off the graph, Hindus,
jihadists, evangelicals and Jews, the odd.
Live and let live, but all fair game to bait.
We bear with those of even weirder views:
our C of E that cannot quite believe in God,
but love his children; this we can forgive.

'Play fair' we say 'give everyone their due.
Be sure you never try to jump the queue,
and Britain's Allsorts nations welcome you.'

Nick Leach

HUMPTY-DUMPTY

Humpty-Dumpty sat on a wall,
Humpty-Dumpty had a great fall,
He really shouldn't have been there at all,
According to Health and Safety.

Humpty was sat on a wall made of bricks,
Acting the fool and doing silly tricks,
Impressing his mates, showing off to the 'chicks',
Ignoring Health and Safety.

When Humpty fell off he landed right on his head,
When the medics arrived, they thought he was dead,
But he opened one eye, looked up and he said,
'You'd best not tell Health and Safety!'

For months after Humpty's little disaster,
He was laid up in hospital, covered in plaster,
'He's in bits,' said a nurse, when somebody asked her,
'He keeps on about Health and Safety.'

They put him together again, apart from one leg,
Which was slightly askew, and held on with a peg,
For the rest of his life Humpty was a cracked egg,
Cos he ignored Health and Safety.

An 'ad' on the tele said, 'Are you in pain?
Had an accident at work, for which you weren't to blame?'
So Humpty gave them a call and put in a claim,
They sent a man from Health and Safety.

The chap went to the wall and then had a fit,
Said, 'Is that the place where you used to sit?'
Humpty said, 'I fell off, I was only there for a bit.'
That didn't impress Health and Safety.

He then said to Humpty, 'Can you tell me why,
You were sat on a wall that is plainly too high?
With no safety equipment; you're lucky you didn't die,
You shouldn't ignore Health and Safety.'

He then said, 'I'm sorry, but your claim is rejected.
There are so many rules your wall sitting neglected.'
Well, it wasn't much more than Humpty had expected,
They are strict in Health and Safety.

Humpty still passes the wall now and then,
Though he has vowed he will not sit upon it again,
Not after all the grief from the H and S men
He's had enough of Health and Safety.

And now on the wall where Humpty once sat,
They've stuck up a notice that tells people that:
'If you sit on this wall you must wear a hard hat.
Thank you. Health and Safety'.

John Morris

ON THE SHORES

Suppose this is the last song
before the lights go out
before the waxwings melt away
across the greedy clouds . . .

Would you still look away
turn on the radio
Would you weave a whisper aloud
so that the sirens don't get to know?

Suppose this is the last draft
before they tear it away
before meanings turn to words again
till all the whites grow grey . . .

Suppose this is the last voice
before they bury it deep
before the moonskin ripens it all
for the poison seeds . . .

Would you still look away
till all the blood grew cold
till all the birds had flown away
and all the lies were told?

They'll come in droves
they'll take you too
and you'll never get to know
how right was the pain you left
many shrieks ago . . .

Avishek Parui

GOING TO THE MOVIES

The moving picture speaks,
and having spoken moves on
to haunt the creative mind,
play with words on the tongue
that may (or may not) paint
pictures of thought others may
(or may not) be invited to see,
interpret as we (or they) intend,
only to subtly, discreetly, let it drop
in a history bin

The moving picture captures
and having captured demands
its captives consider if we're
but slaves to its fictions or privy
to what goes on in those murky
corners of reality we are all free
to access any time but prefer
someone else take a closer look,
and clean it up without too much ado
about nothing

The moving picture speaks,
and having spoken moves in
on the senses if only to see
what (if any) effect on emotions
kept under wraps for fear
we betray aspects of selfhood
that may be misconstrued
as weaknesses where we'd rather
wear our strengths on sleeves frayed
at the edges

Compelled to join forces once
a moving picture has said its piece
and moved on, inner sight
asking of the inner ear what it has seen,
agreeing they feel uneasy
for having been given a taste
of untouchables cast out
by croc tears and canned laughter . . .
Oh but let's just call it entertainment
and forget all about it?

Roger N Taber

MELANCHOLY TIME OF YEAR

It's that melancholy time of year
Thoughts consumed amidst festive cheer;
Dulcet sound of choirs singing
To the distant chime of sleigh bells ringing.

As snowflakes fall in the chilled night air
Excited children are everywhere;
Trying to sleep, tucked in their beds,
Eagerly awaiting the day ahead.

What about the ones who'll cry,
As they open their eyes to question why?
Santa didn't leave a gift . . .
Despite them writing a simple list!

As dawn breaks on Christmas morn'
The day Jesus, our saviour was born . . .
Take a moment to understand,
The folk who yearn to hold a hand.

Innocent tears that will go unheard;
They won't taste a yuletide bird . . .
The elderly ones left all alone
Without someone, to even phone.

Dreams get lost along the way
And aspirations go astray . . .
For some life just isn't fair
And people around, seem not to care.

So, at this melancholy time of year
Take time out from your festive cheer,
Say a prayer for those in need
For they're the ones . . .
With hearts that bleed.

Jane Gill-Wilson

THE CREAM CRACKER MAN

He was someone's uncle – that didn't excuse it
did you say eccentric?
The blackened terrace house, with its twenty-three steep steps,
was suffocating beneath orange-hued packs of Jacob's 'Original and Best'
(must be Jacob's) Cream Crackers,
shortly abbreviated to JCC, this didn't reduce the volume.
Crumbs, I never saw so many.
No butter or marg to be had mind – a dry cream cracker junkie's heaven in there.

The cheaply chic Co-op assistants didn't bat an eyelid
when he blinded them with orange.
A few had started wearing shades – the posers,
the 'claim damages under any conditions' types,
union members: 'Fill in a Health and Safety form.'
What a farce. Try it.
Alert Social Services to his singular diet.

What's the crime in shopping?
He holds up the queue.
Go on then, have a go at him
quiz an elderly man on his shopping habits
be diplomatic
he was at Ypres – no JCCs there.
'Oh, excuse me Mr So and So, cream cracker hoarder,
you bought a boxful yesterday (twelve packs, 360 crackers)
did you forget or are you going crackers?'
Don't help him on his way!

Swap to liquorice allsorts:
Colourful box, chewy, higher calorie,
kiss of death for diabetics.
Get a life, study dietetics.

Collect Penguin books?
for their looks? (they may be orange)
A doddle to store, worth more.
JCCs and Penguins
made for each other but lost in the process
a good marketing ploy
a colour-coded hobby.

Maybe he eats JCCs whilst engrossed in a first edition.
So, he's the culprit: crumbs between pages, I hate him.

Epilogue
We found no Penguin books, his niece and I
he'd made a will,

donated his JCC collection, some vintage, to the niece.
She felt they were of sentimental value.
Me: 'Dump them!'
Niece: 'No! They're his lifetime's work.'

Appears to be hereditary I'd say.
The niece inherited more than a piece from the uncle.
I can't look another JCC in the eye,
as for Penguin books – take a running jump.

Catherine Parker

SHIMMERING GOLD

Our lives are rainbows.

Sunny days are full of laughter,
Sweet and melodic
Like the birds in the blue.
Eyes sparkle, serene and sincere
As though they are dappled
With the pale evening stars.

When the clouds gather above,
Our feet shuffle
Through streets of murmurs,
Those same eyes dull and mature
Whilst observing the ground below,
Wishing away the coming storm.

On the day the cloud breaks,
Shattering rain falls
In torrents of screaming hail,
Pelting at trembling, chilled frames
With the bitter thunder and lightning
Of childhood nightmares and pain.

When our exposed skin shivers,
Soaked straight through
With endless torment and suffering-
Shadows shelter us from the sky's tears,
A hand turned over our halo heads,
The makeshift leaf a helping hand.

Our lives are rainbows.
With a glint of gold.

Sam Jane King

ODE TO COFFEE

O calming, caffeine-filled coffee
You have slain the beasts named Tired and Stroppy,

You comfort poor souls who are cursing and yawning
As they hurry to work in the early morning,

Against drowsiness how bravely you fight
For students working late into the night
Aiming for that deadline with all their might.

But are you truly the saviour of the morning?
Some say 'Coffee is bitter and boring!'

'Confine it to those dull, over-priced cafes
That sell their mochas and milky lattes!'

Some scorn and ask 'What on earth is Dirty Chai
And which mad person concocted the Green Eye?
Lapsang and Earl Grey are the drinks you should buy!'

In Starbucks, you have many a name
So many, in fact, it drives people insane
As they try to pronounce them in frustrated vain,

Still, the early riser would be lost without you
And this is a well-known fact denied by few,

With your warm, mellow taste and lively kick
You are the only drink people should pick,

For a single sip many would travel far;
A god, a saviour – both these things you are.

Jasmin Jackson

BLINDED

In the shattering silence of the night,
The fairies cast magic to and fro,
While children are blinded by holy light.

The moon tries to climb to the bright sun's height,
While monsters creep out of secret hollows
In the shattering silence of the night.

Above the stars dance, though some try to fight,
And old oaks guard the young saplings that grow,
While children are blinded by holy light.

A man-thing explodes, the sparrows take flight,
And squirrels hide by the nest of the crow,
In the shattering silence of the night.

Adults dribble off to rooms out of sight,
The spirits attack with a willow's bow,
While children are blinded by holy light.

Angels watch the world as the souls ignite,
And show them the path in feathers of snow,
In the shattering silence of the night,
While children are blinded by holy light.

Ashton Cooper-Swann

LIFE'S MAGICAL MOMENTS

To wake up in the morning and see the rising sun,
To feel the rain upon my face and watch the birds have fun,
To hear the first dawn chorus as things begin to grow,
The vibrancy of spring flowers as March winds start to blow,
The first sight of the swallow, young ducklings on the pond,
An array of fragrant blossom where blue tits start to bond,
For moments of pure magic, you needn't look too far,
Even in the darkness, the brightness of a star,
For nature is most wonderful, there's nothing to compete,
I'm happy with the little things they make my life complete.

Jennifer Melbourne

HER LOCAL VALENTINE'S DAY

Where in mi lyf roar yoo hunie
Coz it'z empti and no flunny
Eatch noit sitton peelin laranges
On mi oan yawnon ot the telly
Woil stranin to suck owt the jangy joos

Where ar yoo wen I nead yoo
Blecoz it'z the tymm of vantissy
Where yoo brin mi toclats and Flewros
Fer the Valentines evonin
But instod I gut no compliny

The jangy joos has splutod in mi aye
So dewnt wolly is not coz I cwy
An noxt yar wol gera Toclat one
Awlso sun ov lem plostock Flewros
Blecoz is loik weeding a tweep mlagozian

Tom McDougall

FOR THE LOVE OF

The corrupt culture of humans makes you sick,
The love of the colour green
The idea that being the head constitutes a right to take something that belongs not in your hands but in others.

Voted in but never voted out
Selling sweet lies, talking beautiful tales, promising false truths,
Seeing money rather than the people behind.

Simply solutions, complicated reactions.
A country with most but representing a little, how could this be?
Maybe it's ignorance, greed, or maybe it's both wrapped in a box of self.

Head of army, commander in chief, great leader
turned into a selfish money-hungry thief,
With rooms where money runs but runs to no one.

Cries from the decrepit harvest,
From the empty bloated stomachs,
From the failing bodies,
Cries which fall on deaf ears.

Rachel Faturoti

HUMAN DOUBT

It is a late midsummer's afternoon, 4.00pm,
he has the fear spiralling inside him.
He cannot control it.
He worries that something, is going to go wrong,
he questions people sitting at each lonely corner,
asking them what would they ask? What should I reply?
He is trembling like a freshly,
made wobbly strawberry flavoured jelly.
His tiny beads of sweat are leisurely pacing,
down from the top of his head till they,
fall gently on the ground leaving tiny puddles of anxieties.
He takes a glance at the time waiting,
for the big hand to pass 5:00,
his tiresome eyes focused on only the clock,
tapping his weary foot up and down,
waiting for the hours to pass quickly and the day to end.
His stomach is growling with agitation,
like a hungry grizzly bear,
waiting to feed, to exonerate the stomach pains.
There is silence, no whispers,
just the reverberation of the endless clicking of pens,
the birds chirping outside,
the noise of rustling magazine papers.
His confused mind is blocked with boundless,
thoughts not knowing what to do like tangled up wires,
each noted at the back of a Panasonic 10 inch TV.
Its now 5:30, the sun is setting down, he's still pending,
he watches the people down below him through,
the clear transparent glass square,
all hurrying to catch the red 60 bus.
He hears the sirens and observes the police cars,
ambulances rushing to get to their target.
He sighs with a little relief knowing that,
he isn't in that position,
he hasn't been caught by them or lost any,
freedom by defying the law.
He has no apprehension of what he saw looking,
through the shining glass.
Then someone comes out and strolls,
progressively out of the building with a smirking smile.
It is a late midsummer's evening, 6pm,
at that moment he is called into the interview room.

Neelam Shah

THINGS AREN'T ALWAYS WHAT THEY SEEM

Be careful when you look at me,
As things are not always what you see,
This happy, bright facade I have erected,
Is what keeps me safe and protected.

I would not suffer you to see,
The pain some days inside of me,
I would not presume to make you feel bad
Because today I'm feeling sad.

Just be mindful how you speak,
As in places my facade is weak.
Then it takes great time to paper over the cracks,
So I can get my happiness and serenity back.

So please be careful not to break
My facade that took so long to make.
Because I like the person I am trying to be.
The happy, friendly and secure me.

The me that's not afraid,
To dance smile, laugh and sing,
I love to smile at people and say
Hope you have a lovely day.

Cindy Faulkner

LINES ON OVID: 'METAMORPHOSIS: BK VIII: 183-235'

Those words which we had so carelessly caressed the night until night was all,
They have haunted us, exorcised, now the claw scratching burden of freedom,
Phrases so tangled in our torments there were some admissions to the asylums,
She a frost-rigid Aphrodite huddled in the corner an enigma with amphetamine,
Icarus' madness was that of a youth fleeing a flame from drunk with fire father,
Burn and get burnt, you do when you fly high and then touch the Sun to plunge,
Those potions of ascent and descent were worms in graves of a fathomless sea,
'Let me warn you, Icarus, to take the middle way, in case the moisture weighs
down your wings, if you fly too low, or if you go too high, the sun scorches them.
Travel between the extremes.'
The wanderers of those oceans of bewildered unconscious have turquoise eyes,
So occasionally he glances up from pen and paper and peeps around that book.

N S Pearce

GROWTH FROM SPEED

Growth from speed could come at a cost,
Folks of the future may not know what is lost,
With no knowledge of nature,
No desire to hold,
The values,
Not money,
Of those who are old,

Do young minds know better,
Or is destruction the way?
For hard paths to no future
Get wider each day,

As young minds get older,
Will their wisdom unfold,
A route to protect them,
And their valuable world?

Gloria Dales

THE CHILD THAT COULD HAVE BEEN MINE

The child that could have been mine,
The thoughts sends shivers down my spine,
For what I think we could have done,
But getting rid of you was not that fun,

To you I would have been a dad,
But killing you made everyone glad,
I got told it was for the best,
That's when the tightening came in my chest,

Never to hold you in my arms,
Never to teach you all my charms,
Never to kiss you and tell you I love you,
But know I'm always thinking of you,

But death will come to us all,
Maybe in Heaven we can play ball,
In Heaven we will meet for the first time,
I just hope you will forgive me and let me call you mine.

Wayne Clarke

THE WORLD AT MY FEET

I live in an impoverished world yet I don't try to change it
I have enough food to eat yet I discard it
I have the perfect home yet I try to escape it
I have a place to sleep yet I don't respect it
I have a bright future yet I don't try to attain it
I am a developed country citizen yet I don't appreciate it.

Ahad Mahmood

POLYCEPHALY

No magic will ever replace
God's greatest illusion that people have one face.
The surface is where deception is ignited
And why honesty is always requited.

A single cover misleading everyone
Luring trust and affection in a quilted con.

Born from the Hydra people grow
Pretending to be someone else in a well-rehearsed show
This was true of the screen goddess Marilyn Monroe.

With no Hercules to slay the demon
People will continue to commit treason
With a head for every single situation
Perhaps we should have our reservations.
The God of beginnings and transitions
Even Janus has been lost in translation.

Two faces embodying treachery
Placing every interaction in jeopardy
A corrupt smile created to misguide
A mask allowing integrity to hide.

Polycephaly is a deadly weapon
Preventing people from entering the gates of Heaven.
The underworld waits with Cerberus at the entrance
Passing judgement and delivering sentence.

Stacey Reay

THE BOY WHO WOULD BE KING

He was one of those people who wouldn't be famous –
Spencer King – until after he was dead.
One of those people who won't talk on the telephone
Unless he's home alone, and even then he has to pace.
He wouldn't have many friends but those that
He did found him intense and opted for just that.
He was one of those people who saved up for the great days
For Wednesday comic book day
Only to spend it all on knick-knacks and Pacman at noon.
One of those people who spoke too soon,
Known as 'The Hand' as it was always in the air –
Not with abandon or recklessness care,
Nor with an answer for a question for the teacher in question
But a question
'Why is it at the best times in life we are left without a camera close at hand?'
And no one understood because no one knew Spencer King
The boy who uses bookmarks and rides the bus alone,
The boy who would think nothing to busk with his trombone,
Just because he can.
No one understood because no one knew,
No one knew the boy underneath the question
Other than the boy who should've went to a better optician;
Because his sight was blurred.
And he couldn't see through the thick-lensed haze
At the boy in front of him their opinions had made.
He saw more than the snapshot of a generation
Or rather, he saw less.
And he understood the question from the boy in question
And raised his hand to become 'The Hand Two point Zero'
To follow in pursuit of what Spencer King showed:
A tenacity to adore information overload.
'That way, things can be remembered for what they really were and not just what
They appeared to be.' And he understood:
Writing his name on walls would only serve
To distance himself from his goal.
In pictures on walls and framed epitaphs,
Let clematis and ivy frame those frames –
And throw him a quadrat. It's less permanent.

Chris Moore

ELEMENTAL

(To be read out at my funeral)

I dwell on the earth I live in the air
I'm always around and yet never there
Existing in water the fire in the sky
This spirit of nature is never denied

My body's the planet on which you now stand
And all that's upon it was so neatly planned
Rejoice in your life for all that its worth
Enjoy to the fullest your short time on Earth

My breath, is the light wind that ruffles your hair
And whispers life's secrets that hang on the air
Revering my freedom I travel at will
Through yon distant valleys, and over the hills

My soul is the fire that follows each night
That warms up the planet and bathes it in light
For justice and truth and love in your hearts
The strength of our union no evil can part

My tears are the raindrops that so softly fall
Sweet music of life how clear is the call
Cascading down mountains as river and stream
Replacing dry deserts with acres of green

I dwell in the forests no longer alone
Remembered by many in circles of stone
A rock for my pillow the earth is my bed
And the starlit heavens right over my head

Tony Crowther

ON THE ROAD TO FUTURE HAPPINESS

Fork in the road – signpost bears
two place names, one lying east,
the other west; one destination
is called Hope, the other Despair.
Which way will you go, which path
shall you take? Think carefully.

You need to snap out of misery
for once you start off down that
road there's no end to it, no place
to get off, stop or divert; its logical
conclusion is Despair which isn't
even a town, just a bottomless pit.

Instead, get on the road to future
happiness and joy for once you set
off down that road, never looking
back, none can stop you moving
forward in your life with open arms
embracing whatever is to come.

Roar ahead, surge towards a life of
future happiness, untold treasures
invited into your life through the
power and force of positive thinking,
that strange, magnetic attractor
of nature's beneficent laws.

Mat Turner

HOLES

We live like the machines we build,
The world is slowly stripped of its emotions,
The chairman sits,
The workman stands,
But both will have a day they won't remember.

One person digs a hole,
Another fills it up again,
The third man stands and watches,
Whilst fourth is getting paid for jobs,
He didn't even do.

But all of them will come to rest,
Beneath the feet of people that replace them,
And then the process but repeats itself:
A candle's lit;
It burns until extinguished;
A new one is ignited in its place.

And all of this for what?
To satisfy great need our souls,
Possess for digging holes?
The craving that can never be fulfilled,
Until the shovel is in hand,
And earth but trembles at the sight of us?

No.
Most do it for the coin,
And paper they are given for the job,
The same two items that enslave us,
With their hold,
Upon the freedom that we're given in this world.

And yet,
As I but dig a hole,
And wait, in great and pure anticipation,
To fill it up again,
I watch a fellow digger drag his feet,
And drop his shovel deeper in the dump and dreary ground,
Whilst wearing toothless smile upon his tired face.

I asked him: 'Friend,
How do you work so hard,
Yet keep such cheery spirit?'

To answer me,
He placed a picture in my hand,
Which details, lit by setting sun,

Revealed his answer to me:
'They are the reason why,
And this is but the means to be with them.'

It was a picture of his daughters,
His light in dark and gloom,
The reason why no shovelful,
Will ever place him in the boredom's tomb.

He put it back,
As slowly and as tenderly,
As sleeping child is put to rest,
And picking up his ragged tool,
He carried on his downwards decent.

Our world is often very bleak and full of sorrow,
But all it took is one man's ray of joy,
To reignite my faith in true love's power,
And look ahead to a much happier tomorrow.

Nikolai Holding

FLANDERS FIELDS

In Flanders Fields the poppies grow,
In neat copies,
Row upon row.
Signalling the death of true heroes,
Never forgotten friend or foe.

In Flanders Fields we start anew,
Like the joy of seeing a rainbow grow,
Or observing drops of dew.

I visited Flanders once before,
The blood of heroes smeared across the floor,
Where the rich red poppies bloom,
For new ones,
There is lots of room.

These poppies grew at the end of the war,
Where all celebrated across the shore,
The death of war was known worldwide,
There was no need to cry,
No need to confide,
Finally we were all on the same side . . .

Zobia Yasin

CASHKA-ESQUE

And it was there, in the distance.
The tired, dying man, who no one really knows by name.
May be a mirage,
Because the silhouette isn't so sweet.
Especially when you know what it really is . . .
Money.
And that's all it ever is, and was.
Nifty-green, and blue, and purple.
And digits in a statement.
A stolid opportunity.
But Nifty-Green isn't your friend,
And you will burn before he does.
And sometimes he pretends to feed you,
Buy you things you don't really need, or want.
That's his smiling face.
And Nifty-Green does not like the Millipede.
Neither blue nor purple.
And sometimes he promises you things.
Some greedy-green politician with a four-by-four,
And a regular wince at Westminster Abbey.
That's all he's worth,
And so much less, day-by-day.
You see him everywhere,
And he looks different in different places.
The Asuras who never sleeps,
Who you can never touch,
Until you give your life away.
Asuras will treat you the same,
And push your face in the dirt, just like before.
But you accept that . . .
. . . Because it's an abusive relationship . . .
And you can't say no until you break even.
If that's even possible,
For a no-good, talentless hack,
Who's no good for anyone,
And soon you'll crack, and you're not shatter-resistant.
And Nifty-Green will laugh,
Just like he did when the lights went out,

And the water ran cold, and then didn't run at all.
He doesn't care for things like that.
Non-issues.
Because he likes it when you fear for your life.
He likes it when the rice is all that's left.

Thomas Payne-Lawrence

MONSOON BALLAD

I have seen many glorious suns rise,
I have felt the whirl of many festivals.
I have grown strong and wise, as a seeker of truth and beauty.

But today, the sight of young love,
In all its tender beauty,
Has touched me and moved me to tears.

Seated in their presence,
I marvelled at their shy games,
And innocent smiles.
I sought to understand the effortless way in which
Lovers manifest divinity in flesh.

For when the river of love
Meets in perfect harmony
With the river of passion,
The sight is too much to bear.

Though the world welcomes the rain clouds of fortune above,
Today, I watch silently,
As monsoon cataracts gather force,
And besiege the mountains below.

Nandita Keshavan

SON OF A GUN

When I was seven I though I was livin' in heaven
No value for money and never a worry
With holidays laid-on from the St. Vincent De Paul
And the money laid on from the three brass balls
Not forgetting the Sisters of Mercy with their pots of hot rice
It must have been the best years of my life
That was in '65 Elvis had to be one of the greatest men alive
For the older lads that hung around the street corner
Twenty or so versions of Elvis
All with winkle-pickers, drainpipes, leather jackets and greased up heads
I thought my time would never come
I always wanted to join in the fun
Now I'm all shook up, grown up, and greased up
But there's not much fun
When you find yourself on the run without a gun
Should I give myself in?
To those who say I have sinned
Should I learn to bark for the factory boss?
Or should I run against the wind
So I won't hear what they call sinned
It's easy to sin when you bark for the factory boss
So I think I'll buy a gun and stay on the run.

John Walsh

THE HOURGLASS

grains of sand pass like biology
my body ticking like a heart
my love straining like tea
cups stacked like domesticity
a routine ready to be broken
mirrors reflecting misfortune
at the roll of the die
longing for the Sky Plus rewind
Craig David, tracksuit fashion and yo-yos
something missing like a penny
down the side of the sofa
sold at a car-boot
burned at a bonfire
the fireworks and candyfloss melt away
afraid of nothing now
fill my stomach with a hot dog
onion, ketchup; that strong smell
that bright red

Carmina Masoliver

ARE WE READY . . . ?

They said, the war is over
Dark and evil days are gone.
They said, the future is in our hand
A new beginning after the dark end.
They said, no misuse of achievements any more
Going forward wheels of history.

We said, make love no war
Flower power is the manifesto.
We said, give peace a chance
Vietnam has no defence.
We said, anything goes
Liberation on the agenda.

They said, the cold war is over
Ideology has lost its power.
They said, no more discrimination
Political correctness is the solution.
They said, the new millennium is *the* future
Cyberspace open for every one.

We wonder, information age
Still searching for the whole truth?
We wonder, common sense and enlightenment
Fading away or omnipresent?
We wonder, cyberspace – misuse or benefit?
We ask, *are we ready for the 21st century?*

Uwe Danek

A POEM ABOUT LOVE

When I first laid eyes upon you, you took my breath away.
With features of a Goddess, the way you looked just there.
Your flowing locks of auburn, that glint of reddish flame.
Those eyes are pools of honey dew brown.
They melted my heart, they brought me down.

I kneeled before you, enchained in love.
My pulse rate racing like a speeding dove.
You ooze eroticism like an endless drug.
I taste, knowing I will never get enough.

My love for you is like an endless book.
The more you read the more you look.
The more you look the more you read.
The more I want the more I need.

Your love pulsates around my body.
I take a breath you make me quiver.
When you touch I shake and shiver
Your love is like an endless river.

You are my true love, you are my wife.
You are the emblem of my life.
The first kiss that you gave to me.
Our endless love was meant to be.

Our love will last an eternity.
Just as we know it was meant to be.
I am so glad you came into my life.
The promise you made to be my wife.

I now know that you came from above.
Because you showed me what is true love.

Gordon Bailey

THE MOVE

(This poem is dedicated to Tina Peasland. Her move is the subject of my poem.)

Moving is stressful, that is what they say.
Strategy and planning, this will always pay.
Labelling the boxes, services transferred.
Decorating organised, paper you preferred.
The new abode seems wonderful.
The old is in a state.
You should be set to go quite soon, why then must you wait?
Because I am not ready!
The boxes are not packed.
I just trod on a plastic spade, and gave my knee a whack.
I've records, photos, gifts galore. Not all belong to me.
Hoarders that is what we are in our family.
Two pot dogs black, and white, I can't throw them away.
I'll toss these records in the bin.
Oh no! They'd better stay.
The bed is overflowing, I need somewhere to sleep.
I don't know how it got so full of clothes I'd like to keep.
I've tins, and tools a plenty on which to stub a toe.
I've double of just everything.
Something has got to go.
Hats from down the ages.
Why did I buy that dress? The corner I just tidied, now's a ruddy mess.
Tina take a moment, you really don't feel well!
My nostrils now are filling. What's that funny smell?
The cooker is on fire. Don't panic just keep calm.
Turn it off, fan the smoke, wildly wave your arm.
Events occur distract me. Disturb my line of thought.
No wonder I'm a mental wreck. I'm tired, and rather fraught.
My fella tries to help me. He's running east and west.
He's got a lot of patience, as yet he's not got vexed.
As, and when I finally go, I'll sit, and just relax.
Or maybe read a mag. or two, and give my legs a wax.
A person who is organised, and moves without a hitch.
Must be either Superman, or Samantha the white witch.
I wish I had a nose that twitched so I'd not have to worry.
Life is full of problems, work. Nothing more than hurry.
So don't tell me to plan my move, to plot each small event.
The person who came up with that is nothing short of bent.
I'll do it all my own way just you wait, and see.
T. The whirling Dervish.
The small demented bee.

Christine Stafford

FREE AT LAST

I went to the circus some time in January,
And stepped through the curtains of the giant marquee.
As I entered the tent, there was some kind of cat,
With black and orange stripes all over its back.

The creature was more agile than anything before,
As it jumped through a hoop, landing gracefully on the floor.
It flew with such ease through the colourful rings,
Anyone would think that this cat had wings!

But if you looked long and hard into its gaze,
You would soon realise it was lost in a maze.
It didn't know whether to run or hide,
Or to stay in its cage, locked up and tied.

So that's why I did it, right after the show,
I unlocked his cage and let the cat go.
He ran like the wind, leaving his past,
He was finally free, free at last.

Joanna Brás-Goldberg

MANTRA

When the mind of a man becomes divided the man becomes divided.
What a divided man sees, his hands unmake.
Such a man no longer knows himself.
The walls of his mind become as water,
allow distractions to invade, multiply.

A man must have purpose, for by the weight of his purpose
is a man defined.
A man without purpose is without definition.
To lack definition is to lack function.
He exists in opposition to himself
and the knowing of this divides him further.

There must be balance in all things, for strength lies in knowing oneself.
Through the knowing of oneself comes clarity.
Through clarity, focus can be directed and applied.
There cannot be two skies.

Jake Saw

CHILDHOOD PHOTOGRAPH

The photo is in black and white.
It dates from the early fifties.
This might be its diamond jubilee year.
It shows a young boy
on the lawn in front of a semi.
He peers, squinting into the sun
and the camera lens.
And behind the camera?
His mam? A friend? Not his dad.
His dad won't be home from the pit yet.
By the boy's feet, a dog relaxes,
tongue lolling in the heat.
The dog, a smooth-haired fox terrier,
is lean, alert, intelligent.
It's the boy who is chubby with puppy fat.
He will cry for a week when his dog is run over.
He will cry less when his dad dies
or even ten years after that, for his mam.
He does not know that very soon
he will be me.

Phil Poyser

BLISS

You pull him close
He pulls you closer
You hold him tight
He holds you tighter
You gasp
His grasp falters
You clutch at him in desperation
You feel his embrace regain its tightness
Thoughts of him penetrate every inch of your mind
Your brain, drained of this world
The present becomes a distant memory
As you move into a place of your own
Where the distance
Between you and him
Becomes
Nonexistent.

Ghazal

SOBER SOCIETY

My friends don't understand the morals
Of people like me who don't drown their sorrows.
And who don't seek the answers at the end of their beer
Because I know better than to hide from fear.

The night grows long and my patience short
With peer pressure that I have persistently fought;
I hate being labelled a spoilsport
Simply because alcohol is my last resort.

But still I have fun in the absence of absinthe.
With no dependency on drunken nympths
Or alcohol to provide a thrill
As I know that mere adrenaline will.

The speakers thump and shake the ground
Whilst people express themselves to the sound
Of 'dubstep', 'pop', 'rap' or 'soul'
Or 'drum and bass' and 'rock and roll'.

People raise their glasses and voices alike
Partying hard, long into the night;
Drinking heavy, no need to sup
Spirits, they fall to the floor and sober up.

A shameful routine for one to act
With little use of 'sense' or 'tact',
And different understandings of right and wrong
As anything goes from dusk 'til dawn.

How many times must I repeat myself
To the stereotypes who result in stealth
To spike my beverage, coz they don't think that I fit in;
Because I sit out and do not sin.

Darren James Lee

Y

Forgotten society and broken morally
A world led by hapless invertebrate,
Complete conspiracy full of mystery,
Those in charge there uncontrollably,
Stupid policy shadows the reality,
Follow those who lead the anarchy,
Corrupt authority can't control humanity,
A tourist attraction is that of royalty,
True perjury by leaders calmly,
Their lies and wrongdoing hidden in secrecy,
Childhood's unhappy adulthood goes badly,
Unless part of the middle class family,
Heroes collectively treated so terribly,
Support is needed for Air, Sea, and Army,
Small possibility a chance of liberty,
Console your dreams in personal sanctuary,
Endless serenity craved for eternity,
Do no spoil the mindless tranquillity,
Pointless celebrity a list full of many,
Keeping out the true who'll die a wannabe,
Blind fury, rage goes crazy,
Unbelievable they got the opportunity,
Music philosophy not what it used to be,
Institutionalised like all in the top forty,
Listen closely not too distantly,
And revealed is the lack of vocal ability,
Useless lyrically others write accordingly,
For those with no depth or creativity,
Consumer strategy advertising technology,
Keep up the rat race for the must have trendy,
Trapped psychologically, narrow minded majority,
Their money stolen to fund war criminality,
Strange normality and fake quality,
Driving minds into insanity,
Mixed nationally, and uncontrollably,
When can we will see this worlds just one big country.

Kemal Lee Bakici

WELCOME TO CUMMERLAND

What fettle?
Thou's in Cummerland now, and verra welcome.

Oor bit's a grand spot,
Wid many a mile of rolling green, and sec silver streams
An rivers, where blue kingfishers dive and dippers bob.
We've got greet big wild meadows where bumble bees
Work through the wild thyme, like eager politicians
Shaking hands, kissing babies.

Oor bit's a grand spot,
Wid sec harbours that yance brought in slaves,
Rum and ore and shipped out coal and steel.
We've got the seaside: pebble beaches and glorious rippled
Sand: where t' wind brings the smells of the sea;
And we treat oorsels to fish an' chips, and candyfloss
Or an Allonby ice cream.

Oor bit's grand spot,
Made o' marsh and mountains; forests and fells,
Where, by t' lake's shore, nature's beauty is doubled on reflection.
Whativver the weather, rain or shine, torrent or tempest
There's allus summat t' see, an' allus someone ready for a good craic
Ower a cup- a- tea, an (like as not) a lyle bit cake wid rum – butter or honey,
Canny hospitality.

Oor bit's a grand spot,
Where Whitehaven's 'Tall Ships' tek oor breath away;
Wigton bustles : speaking its own language: on market day
And at Appleby Fair when caravans arrive, horse drawn, and
Time is stripped away, as hooves echo, wefted wid laughter,
Alang cobbled streets.
In Carlisle: on silken Sunday afternoons: sunshine guilds
Oor ancient stones ,as castle and cathedal sit togither,
Companiable as dowagers ower tea, and listen as the
Sweet and mellow tolling of the bells call us t' Evensong.
Oor bit 's sec a blessed spot.

Sue Jones

MY FAMILY TREE

When researching up their ancestry
Royalty can trace their family tree
Though their ancient limbs may intertwine
One small defect blights their grapevine!

When designing up their heraldry
Dynasties are traced back to the Goth
Thoroughbred their bloodlines seem to be
There's one branch they'd like to chop off!

So, forgive me, there's a family secret to confess
About the family weakness that I wish we could suppress!

Granny's drunk again!
Drunk on pink Champagne
She's gone insane
Now thinks she's John Wayne!
It's inhumane
Her blood's high octane!
Can't we restrain
Dignity regain?
Though she acts bizarre
She's still Grand-mama!

Grandpa's 'high' again!
Turn a blind eye again
His new campaign
Swim nude 'cross to Spain!
Dines on Chow Mein
Dressed in Cellophane!
Laughs like a drain
High as a weather vane!
Though he acts bizarre
He's still Prime Minister!

Grandma's fist again
Hit the therapist again!
She's very bruised
And she's been accused!
But I digress
'bout the old Duchess
Punched a princess
Mugged a baroness!
Though we act bizarre
At least we're not *bourgeois!*

So when climbing up your family tree
There's a thing to learn from history
Never sit upon that *barmy* limb
Emigrate and use a pseu-do-nym!

Barley Robinson

THE MUSIC OF THE SPHERES

As planets move around the moon, they, very softly, sing;
Their awe-inspiring music has to it, a truly lovely ring.
Their melodies can be heard in Heaven, way up on high,
But, to human ears, their soft sounds are, very sadly, denied.

The music heard, down on Earth, can never quite compare,
To any of the heavenly music, which is heard way up there.
Only a blessed few, can hear the soft sound of the spheres:
It brings unto them, a sense of total calm, and eternal cheer.

Those who can hear the music, have no mortal form:
They will never ever die, as they were never ever born.
It can not be heard by a soul that is encased with flesh;
By such music, such a soul, can never be impressed.

Heaven is thickly inlaid with stars of the brightest gold:
A truly dazzling sight, for two young lovers to behold.
The milky moon illuminates the weary world down below;
Decorating everything within sight, with a soft, silvery glow.

Such sweet music, coupled with such an amazing scene,
Would create such special magic: a young love's dream.
But mortal lovers who, upon this Earth, still do roam,
Can not hear the music, so have only the view alone.

The cheerful Cherubins, with their eternally clear sight,
Revel in such music, and, in it, find such sheer delight.
Our souls will go to Heaven, when we pass away;
There, resting in peace, our souls will forever stay.

Angela Wybrow

WHISPERING PEN

A door opens
on A4 block.

Lamplight falls
on Page's smooth skin.

She's been waiting
just for *him.*

'What is it?'
Page begins,
her face,
faintly lined,
a blank.

'I love these moments,'
he says,
his shadow over her.

'This *is* my moment for you,
Whispering Pen,'
she muses.

'I just want to say,'
Pen kisses her,
'I'm so glad
you're here
for me.

'If not,
how could I express
the thoughts that come to me
in the middle
of the night?'

Page waits
silently
for him to caress her
once more.

'I mean,' says Pen,
tapping in reflection,
'the thoughts that come
through me.

'When I'm in the flow,
words take me over
and I give myself up
to let them pour out.

'As if I'm held
by something bigger . . .'

Pen hesitates.

'Go on,'
Page murmurs
Feint with longing
For the next touch.

'Sometimes
I s-o-o-o want
to make my mark
on the world!'
Pen jumps on the spot.

'Certainly
you've made your mark
on *me*!' says Page.

His words
written all over her
make her feel
cherished.

The marriage might be brief
ending with her
screwed up,
torn apart.

But . . .

if not discarded,
maybe she'll be
treasured,
wrapped and held
in long-term
significance.

If . . .

Whispering Pen retracts.

Clicks.

Doodles.

'*But then –* '

'Mmm?' says Page,
full of words
she can't express,
only carry.

'Oh, Page!' Pen squiggles.
'I'm making
such a mess!

'If only I could
rub it all out
and start
over again!'

Page flutters;
faintly wrinkles.

Pen draws back.

'Page?' he whispers,
poised for her response.

'What is it, Page?
I can't read you at all!'

Through the web
of dots and blots,
Page smiles.

Despite the mess
she is *so* fond
of its creator.

Now smudged
with ink and tears,
Page sighs for him
who gave her
meaning.

'Dear, *dear* Whispering Pen.
You've more to say
than I can hold.

'But look,
you've made your point;
and now it's time
to turn over
a new leaf.'

'Yes! Oh *yes*!
Page, my darling,
What else can I say?
Except that you were there
when I needed you!'

'My pleasure,'
Page murmurs

(*and my only purpose*,
she thinks;
will anyone
ever look at me
again?)

Page's end,
Pen's new beginning.

His kiss, her last;
his words, hers forever.

Crumpling softly,
Page turns away.

Behind her
on A4 block,
another,
clean and blank,
is waiting.

Lamplight falls
on Page . . .

Two.

Janet White

AT MY MOTHER'S BED

An apparition of
a swirling, unending
conduit of time
containing the
moment each daughter
of my ancestors
kissed their dying mothers,
in succession,
enveloped me and
feeling embraced by
these ancient sisters
I received the courage
to kiss my mother
and say goodbye.

Diane Jardel

SYNTHETIC STABBED MY BLUE PRINT

Touch me with your gutter soap
Blacken me with coals, and parlor blood
Kiss me with kitchen knives and I will drop the milk bottles,
And walk through the glass.

Paper bullets and a handful of rewritten suicide notes
A plastic world that suffocated, fumes that spread like water
Gardens of fake and prim, repression strangled round creepers

A million fumbled shy words, pins that got pushed in too deep
Scars on the deserts and trees that have not grown back their leaves
Bombs of hate streaming through a sky where the moon shines, loyally

Vomit pills and chemical nutrients, children washing in the sewers
Armour tears and a lifetime of praying, there is no passion
And if should falter here, now, would you walk on by?

Powered marble – a dream that never won
White horses and beached whales, crying, shrieking,
Resonating in my ears

Each breath I take is poison, each step I take I am weakening
Aching for a time where the world was beautiful
With green and the fresh smell of the rain

Synthetic stabbed my blue print

Sunset has vanished never to return,
Wax melting in the heat from artificial brightness.
Dripping against the tangy hum.

And crystals scrape mirrors
Spots of scarlet dancing in the reflection,
Everything is so painful, ugly and intense

Hayley Nix

RELATIONS

I saw you, and I walked straight past you.
I had my group of friends, and I laughed at your loneliness.
You resembled any normal Gemma, never Zirconia.
I saw you every day for two years, but never exchanged even the smallest pleasantry, as different sides met alternate minds, but then

it all changed. After four years, all my sore fears were exchanged for laughter.
One lesson, four times a week, with the future seeming bright, as opposed to bleak and with just one wry smile, our eyes met over the room.
Derailed thoughts, with views changing overnight, and desires turning towards the possibility of yourself as my future wife.
For you were a heart stopper, body popper, brain clogger . . . and that's before I said hello.
The stem, strong, the road, long, the bond, tough, and your personality, rough, and I liked it.
I love a bit of banter me.

However, once the yearly period had ended, one had become bored.
You were, once again, that standard Gemma, certainly not 24 carat.
Indeed, problems began as I span in that whirlwind you called 'stages of a relationship'.
I felt nothing from your touch, not even the slightest arousal.
You had become head over heels in love, and thus you had forgotten the wedges. You lacked taste.
Dissolution had contacted us many times, yet you chose not to answer, but I had had enough.
A call was best, a text seemed quite harsh and a visit too emotional, hence it was postponed until the most desirable time available.
After two hours it was complete, far from a fable.
I had fought my way through the supposed jungle of hardship.
My hand was now, and remained to be, closed.
A great man once said, 'you cannot shake hands with a clenched fist', though all of the other things I had done with such fist would surprise you. Yet I will not expose, or exchange blows in a war of words, as memories are reduced to sh*t, and you can keep those turds.

The last day of college came and to see no signature on my polo was no great shame, but from the corner of my eye, I spotted a small teardrop.
I felt it be my duty to speak, as though you may feel the turbulence will never end, clear skies can never be too distant.
An embrace ensued, with all previous grievances pursued, and removed, and thus it seemed a fresh slate.

I decided on a Sunday morning to go shopping with the 'group'.
We spent, but not much.
As we left, I spotted the old Zirconia, and continued to walk, whilst remaining civil and sane.
Fittingly, it began to trickle with rain and it seemed what we had before would never quite be the same.
Clouds grey, not blue, for . . .
I saw you, and I walked straight past you.

Arrondeep Mattu

SHE PUT IT ON ME

Was minding my own business, she snuck up on my blind side.
And displayed confidence that was beyond her years.
Flip me like a coin and had the game in her hands.
Went with it as it caught me by surprise.
I knew she wanted me I could see it in her eyes.
She saw me changing in front of her.
Was doing so in a location that weren't unisex but only meant for boys.
But here surroundings didn't overwhelm her, as she came into this environment with a purpose.
To explore new habitat me.
Flirting is my second tongue and fluent as I have blood coursing through my veins.
I matched her comments and banter and played for service looking for the advantage.
That brief situation ended as a maths equation and there was a exchange of numbers.
Texted and talked constantly like trying to make up lost time.
Did things in public locations.
That would of raised eye brows done behind closed doors.
She was uncharted lands and I was Columbus discovering and conquering all that was beneath me.
Kept what ever this was a secret.
Like I had something to hide or in my mind it suited better to be hidden.
Found pleasure in what she would do to impress me.
Was naked and didn't need to undress me.

Duban Sinclair

SAFETY FIRST

(Poecile montanus: the Willow Tit. Recent steep decline, now Red List)

They're drawn to feed, give sway to Blue Tit, Coal
and Great. Brown back, buff under-parts, black cap;
Willow or Marsh? No notion till you find
the nest, in bole so rotten woodpeckers
have upped and left. While clearing leaves you hear
the snarling chainsaw. Council's pruning dead
wood out, so flailing boughs don't injure folk.
Their homes demolished, birds have flown, perhaps
for good, but does this matter in the scheme
of things, when others neither know nor care?
It's now a country park, access for car
and wheelchair, orange gravel pathways, bins
habitually jam-packed with doggy doos,
by seats, where you can pause and contemplate.

Peter Branson

THAT'S ENTERTAINMENT 2012

Screaming tyres and drugged up drivers
Teenagers hanging in a concrete jungle
50 million people live in complete isolation
Urban renewal makes a desert of your town

Living a lifestyle and eating junk food
An obese family play PC games for exercise
Facebook, Twitter, the internet's calling
A book is something that you leave at school

A too short weekend – pull a sickie on Monday
You dream of something better with more money
But you live on credit with a car unpaid for
And you go on YouTube for a glimpse of life

The night sky is a diamond strewn wonder
But the stars you look at are the ones in 'Hello'
On TV, people are dying and bombs exploding
But you turn to your serial heroes.

Hazel Cartwright

HAPPY BUT NOT SAID

I want to be the one who you wake up next to
I want to be the one who tells you I love you
I want to hold you in my arms
call you my special girl
take you far away,
as far as the eye can see.
and sit you down
on the shore of paradise
and whisper in your ear
'come call me dear,
I shall cure all your fear'

Ashley Stafford

THE HEADY HEIGHTS OF HARIETTA MORGAN

Harietta Morgan gazed within lit TV screen;
Sitting in her faded chair as throne to acting queen;
Dreaming of a bigger break from smaller stage and show;
Something that would not involve her dragging sets in tow.

She got herself an agent, found him drunk against the bar. He promised her the whole wide world
was waiting not too far.
And then one day the phone did ring, her big break had arrived.
She called her friends in earnest, at least those she could confide.

'I can't discuss the part,' she gleaned 'until I get the fee,
But I promise now, one and all that fame will not change me.
The studio is rather small, the budget rather lean;
But I will stand dead centre stage upon that silver screen.'

Celebrating half the night with bucks fizz glass in hand;
The next day her audition call was far from fun or grand.
Sitting on the acting couch, a figure slithered in;
Half artist, half devil with lips that smacked of sin.

The read through was a quick affair and when the reading stopped,
This director from a foreign land allowed with shoulders dropped,
his legs to march upon this girl, yet woman through and through.
'You've got the part; I love your art so filming can ensue.'

The carpet in her run down flat did gather dust in circle;
As spinning round the woven floor, the lines were learnt whilst fertile.
She noticed that in all the acts she played another part.
First one was a farmer's maid, the next a village tart.

When the point was raised at lunch with agent and a beer,
He told her to relax and read, 'More parts mean money dear.'
Settling in with cast and crew was not an easy job.
They'd stare at her performances as human monologue.

Still she liked attention and the camera never left;
Unlike her useless mother who couldn't wait to leave her set.
'Now glare into the camera,' came the orders from the chair.
'Jump and run, slide and shout,' an endless noir nightmare.

The months soon passed as party loomed to celebrate its end.
An experimental movie with Miss Morgan's skills to fend.
The bash was just a drunken mess; her throat felt rather sore.
Growling, deep and husky, then found what her drinks were for.

Her agent was indeed a sham and had been from the start;
Plying her with cocktails and a special pill for heart.
Her levels of testorone had doubled overnight.
The shaving now was quite morose and gave her morning's fright.

'The final scene is yet to come,' crooned assistant with elixir.
'You had to undergo this change to finish studio picture.
The final part involves you playing a role of different sex;
And once it's all within our can we'll break your male hex.

'The pills that can reverse your state are ready to receive,
But you must play the game to fill, a part just named as Steve.'
Terrified of failure and remaining stubble rash,
She agreed to next day's final shoot so as not to end up trash.

But even in the limo home her hormone gripe was moral rage.
How could they take advantage of her fame-fuelled trail ablaze.
It said so in her tight contract but she'd not cared to look.
She'd have to change quite medically to allow her off their hook.

When finally she went to play said Steve on centre mark,
She found that at the studio the lights were glaring dark.
The bailiffs had removed all the pictures from the walls.
The studio was bankrupt and the boss declined her calls.

Now Harry Etta Morgan spends his days within his home.
He runs an advice service for the ones that glory moan.
The lesson that was learnt by Harry haunts his memory.
'I promise you, one and all that fame will not change me.'

Nathan J D L Rowark

THE SIGHTS AND SOUNDS OF JUBILEE

Jockeys jostling, horses hustling,
Colours blazing, royals gazing;
Royals boating, barges floating,
Tugboats towing, all hands rowing;
Royal feasting, loyal toasting,
Locals lunching, street kids munching;
Some stars rocking, others rolling,
Someone rapping, royals clapping;
Beacons beaming, lanterns gleaming
Fireworks flaring, night lights glaring;
Music playing, people praying,
Choirs singing, church bells ringing;
Jubilating, celebrating,
The Queen's Diamond Jubilee.

David Lougher

CANDLES

Ebony twists wrapped in moonlight and stars
Frame lines, contours and flashing russet lamps
Which light whene'er smiles settle
And scarlet flushes flare to my words.

As the strongest lighthouse beckons sailors home,
I meditate in orbit around the strongest sun.
As you emanate love and light and life,
I paint a poet's picture of a heart's explosion.

As sunsets are layered in colours of heliotropes and indigoes,
Such is love, as layers form in lips and red and fragrant rose
In kisses shared, sunsets gaze upon and promises whispered before bedtime,
In the shouting, the sighing and the inevitable good-night kiss.

Flowing of cool water on fervent flames wash over
As kisses are delivered in delicious envelopes.
Smooth, luscious frivolity as the moon rejoices above
And darkness hides the grins and blushes.

Glowing candles melt and meld forever
As wind blows in
And rain roars
And the soil soaks.

Alexandra Krendel

UNTITLED

The person I shared my hopes and dreams with
Is now just the person who shares my bed

We would have been appalled at what we have become
We would have said we would never let it happen
We wouldn't have believed it

Our fire is burning out now
Though it will never go out, just fade away
Fade away to body heat in the night

But still I count myself lucky
Some people sleep in separate rooms

Rosanna Bennett

SCRUTINISED

The future is unclear,
looks as dark as the past.
Staying up all night,
thinking, dreaming, hoping.
Life seems like a struggle,
everything slipping fast.
More and more and more,
moping, just moping.
Why me?
I always wonder,
under constant inspection.
if only, if only.
The days are so clouded,
so much rain and thunder.
Crying out for help.
I'm lonely . . . lonely.

Kara-Jayne Smith

PRECIOUS STONE

Light filters through
The broken glass
Of my heart.
Threatens to shatter
As the shine intensifies

This is the effect
You have on me

No matter how hard I try
To reduce this reaction
I have no way of stopping
My crystal sleeve
From cracking under pressure

Leaving my heart bare
Free to all advances
And all the injuries
That will soon follow

Zoë Elson

THE LAST KISS

This will be our last kiss
We both know there's nothing more
All our kisses have turned to shadows
There's no true love here anymore

A million stars and rainbows
Have faded gently into mist
We're drifting away, not falling
As if we've never, ever kissed

All that remains is friendship
It's better by far than hate
To have shared so many memories
That's not so bad a fate

Please be happy, please find love
I hope someday I'll find it too
Until then let's just remember
There was love between me and you

This last kiss is the sweetest
All that was, that might have been
The love and life we had together
A parting gift to set us free

Carolyn Fittall

SUNSETS

Diffuse sunset of pastel china blue,
Golden marbling beautifying the hue,
Feathery white diagonals of vapour trails,
Linger dying a distant as daylight pales.

Blanket skyscape lilac tinted,
Escaping failing sun not even hinted,
Falling light eerily subdued,
Tonight's sunset barely construed.

Inlaid bronze clouds shining majestic might
Glide stately; heavy purple quilt brings the night,
The sky taken, cajoled prematurely to slink
Into its slumber; fading edges of foaming pink.

Andrew Rimmer

CREATION FOR CURRENCY IS CORRUPTION

I think about telling my dad
that I've had another piece published,
but I know what he'll say;
'Did you get paid for this one?'
and I'll tell him no, you have to pay your dues,
I'll even suggest with some degree of optimism,
which is rare for me, that it will all work out
in the end, but then he'll give me that look;
the one that deftly swoops behind me, grabs me
by the throat, and desecrates it
until my Adams apple is spitting pips onto the kitchen floor.
I want to tell him
that creation for the sole purpose of currency
is fundamentally corruption, that it's his kind of attitude
that has devalued money to a numerical system
stamped onto an innocent white screen
that has absolutely
no
meaning – to
anyone,
I want to tell him
that most people need a paper bag
with a packet of valium, or a bottle of Jack inside
to stop the pain, but not me – I have a pen, some paper,
and a vivid imagination.
But I know that once I finish my little pep talk
he'll still be giving me that same old look,
so I don't tell him when I get published, and I never
get that look, and perhaps we are both better people
because of this.

Craig Taylor-Broad

A.P.I.N.N.A.N.

So this is me, slightly sober. Smiling.

Casting glances like nets at the quivering giants
Holding beating feathers in their hair, golden green.
'Home is for the wholesome' written in Braille on their bark.
And belief fills me to the brim as the warbled words burst forth
From bent legs and spread toes: from throats before beaks,
As tongues dance as slack-stringed puppets on a stage overhead.

So this is me, slightly sober. Smiling.
Crowned with flame and wide-eyed . . .
Whilst coarse meadow grass grows between toes,
Growing wild! I scatter-spread alms from empty palms
At brown velvet boughs – whispering understated understanding.
Only the emperors in iridescent skins break my calm.
For I am sugarcane. I am stars.
Catching feelings in plastic jars.

So this is me, slightly sober. Smiling.
Crowned with flame and wide-eyed,
Reaching palms upturned to the furious birds . . .
I dance over streams and run
From all the teen-tigers that've been tamed
by neck-tie nooses, charming cheques, and to office-chairs-chained.
(Whilst those birds) Cast shadows on the sun.
Cloudless, crowned with flame,
Feathers flecked with the fire and soft skin sun-stained.

So this is me, slightly sober. Smiling.
Crowned with flame and wide-eyed,
Reaching palms upturned to the furious birds.
Now their words touch teeth 'til they twinkle . . .

Like slivers of moon pursed over vaporous night.
We speak of dreams long lost to mist encroaching,
Of waves that wash our wishes away in spite,
Of everything we made real in the empty approaching.

Though death and taxes may make us shells,
Some men will forever be ghosts of themselves.

So this is me, slightly sober. Smiling.
Crowned with flame and wide-eyed,
Reaching palms upturned to the furious birds.
Now their words touch teeth 'til they twinkle,
As they swim in streams of liquid light.

So sing furious birds!

Take flight like a thief.
Be everything in yourself, up above and beneath
And spread feathers over eyes
And dark doom-filled skies
And every alley waltz-walked by grey men in grey ties.

So this is me, slightly sober. Smiling.
Crowned with flame and wide-eyed,
Reaching palms upturned to the furious birds.
Now their words touch teeth 'til they twinkle,
As they swim in streams of liquid light
Until I find myself standing in ovation.

Piers Harrison-Reid

IN GENTLER TIMES

In gentler times our bodies touched; our smiles juxtaposed in rare, forgotten moments of oneness.
You, the man whose haunting shadow I'd one day assume and I, the child from whom you'd stray.
In this unspoken way you passed, and I acquired, that wisdom and perplexity that makes the man a man.
Destined to carry and project an inconsistent blend of inner helplessness and bold resilience:
Doubt kept invisible; dependability displayed.
And tenderness, a wire that straddles this divide, is sacrificed to perilous sways between the two.

By deepening furrows through divergent tracks and borne with unforgiving haste we moved
Towards our separate and preoccupying disaffections,
Not understanding if they ever could or did conjoin our thoughts.
But each suspecting that they probably should.
Until is come once more a – final – time when we are side by side.
And maybe in mysterious space 'twixt your unstirring lips and my mouthed prayers
The answer to that question lies.

Peter Taylor

MY CHILD

I raised you to be an adult
not to grow old as I did.

I notice the tramlines on
your forehead I
did not foresee,
the crows-feet cobwebbing
your innocent soul,
the chains of age cornering
your lips, the cracks above.

I wanted to watch your maturity.
I wanted you to succeed in
whatever you undertook,
to find your mirror mate,
to produce my grandchildren.

I was selfish even though I knew
you would settle a different patch
of floor, as fern rhizomes spread under-
ground to uncurl lucid green fronds
in sunlight, apart from the parent.

But mores change, a different world
decrees brand new beliefs and you accept.
You have yet to understand the grand
circle of being, the recurring, returning,
repeated unique wholeness of life.

I stand back, love you whatever and forever.
I learn to adapt within my own knowing
because I understand what's been said forever.
And however you turn out,
for me, you'll do.

Gillian Wallace

COMBAT CAMOUFLAGE

I sit alone as my worried eyes search the trench
I see pain filling their faces as death creates a new stench
I hear the soldiers talk as I continue to look around
They speak of those who are lost and found

My new home is now nothing more than a grave
I wasn't built to act brave
A single tear falls as my motivation disappears
I feel myself going insane due to these pointless fears

I hear the sound of guns hammering in the distance
Being made to fight, what is the point of my existence
Then I hear sounds of bombs screaming and shouting about
I don't want to go, I want to get out

I feel faint as I go over the edge
I can't see a soul as they are camouflaged by this smoke
I start to respond to the incoming fire,
But it's too late now as I hear the afterlife asking me to retire

I feel cold lying in my deathbed of blood
This heavy rain is building a river to carry my body away from this flood
A soldier tries to stop me from falling into the arms of death
But I slip away from reality after I draw my final breath

What is the point of this war?
Why can't things be like they were before?
Who will care for the grieving families?
Why are we blaming the innocent when the government lose?
Once they are gone, who will take control of this power?
And who will be left standing in the final hour?

Stephanie Caldwell

GRIEF - RING OF LOVE

You have taken my heart
and thrown out the key.
I no longer exist.
I exist,
in hell.

White ash tree on Donegal Road
Black buds
Oh that my heart would burst with your green leaf cloud
And not with my grief

You said that you'd loved me all your life
And it was true
You said you'd grown old, loving me,
And that was true

Old waiting for me

I looked with eyes of love.
You turned away.

You saw me afar
Coming through milky way
Through station rainbow dome
The tunneled trees
Coming from distance
At last to your love

You put out the. Light, and then
you put out the Light

out!

Bells' ring o'er the deep
Faint chime in the waves
Sonic love
Of tender sweetness

He has gone my lithe lovely shark
My so beautiful beautiful catch
With his shining scales and silvered loins

O come O come my love to me
Did I not catch you?
You just swim away
With silver loins

False . . . False to your falsing'st heart.
Snow burst on blackthorn
Wild thorn rose

Ruth Finnegan

NO ONE

In the woods
Surrounded by nature
Lost
Alone
No one else to see what I look like
No one can hear my voice
This is what I want
No one to look at me
With judging eyes
A prying stare
Indirectly ruling my life
The choices
The decision
No one to be someone
Then become another person
Conformity
Obedience
Rules
No one to offer undesired opinion
No one to make me feel less
In the woods
Surrounded by nature
Reborn
Unafraid
Brave
No one but the starlight and I

Craig Kenn

BUS RIDE

Filthy day, drizzly grey,
City street, freezing feet,
Aching ears, bus appears.

Dead cold, doors unfold,
Damp fares, clattering stairs,
Here's us, on the bus.

Steamy heat, furry seat,
Stale smoke, dodgy bloke,
Child eats bright sweets.

Engines cough, set off,
Street below, off we go,
Mucky glass, people pass.

Sicky smell, pingy bell,
Bus stops, more shops,
Stop, go, quick slow.

Lights splash, colours flash,
People eat in the street,
Closing shops, bus stops.

Off we go, starting slow
But going faster, zipping past a
Line of trees. No one sees
The haunted park as the dark
Takes all; as the fall
Of the night puts to flight
Frightened day. Run away!
Hide away, hunted day
Who lingers, from the fingers
Of the night, which might
If they get you, never let you
Dawn again. Only darkness then.

Hurtling bus throws us
Through the night. Pray we might,
Racing spark, escape the dark
And killing chill – breathlessly, until
We slow, as we know
Where we are: not far.

All's well. Ring the bell.
Who dares, leap the stairs,
Empty bus, just us.

Doors close, then it goes.
With its light through the night.
Farewell, safe shell. Farewell.

Will Forsyth

NO MORE

You said no more
But
My body will go on living
Though my heart and soul
Will die a thousand painful deaths.
I'll stumble like a fool
As a matter of mindless preservation
To get a foothold on some rocky outcrop
To save me from drowning.
I will feel it ebbing out of me
Love
Channelled like a stream
Condensed and controlled
Becomes almost like a dream.
Never to wake
And like the stream
Inevitably, it will be lost
Swallowed up by the sea.
The sea of life.
And though the body will flounder
Flap upon the shore
My heart and soul will sink
Into the abyss
To belong to no one evermore

John Howe

FOR ANGELIQUE

As I queued in London, the Eurostar late,
she'd watch my bags while I hunted for coffee.
Twenty five? Parisienne?
Rien de flow, la conversation –
peut-etre.

Inching along, a problem with coffee,
without any prompting she carries my easel.
Amour, je sais, *c'est magnétique*:
people would think us *une clique*.

We'd neither seen grass for weeks due to snow,
so I ventured that deserts to die in were *beau.*
Comparing our likes and dislikes she easily
breached the core, the me lying hidden:
she shared some phobias I had suppressed:
thunder and lightning, agreed, caused distress;
a fear of swimming – she'd seen a shark gore;
the wrench to leave one's home and one's pets,
and working at night, when never distraction,
was *bon* and *joie*. Ah *c'est bon interaction*!
Novels were great, but poems less appealed;
Shakespeare a joy, though Zola she loved,
the one about miners her favourite book;
Othello . . . no Lear her number one play;
I noted no make-up, the auburn long hair –
we both loved to sing in choral society –
slight wave over forehead (don't usually stare);
we both like villages more than the city –
but I looked long and deep into two olive eyes –
and I leant as she talked, and she leant as she talked,
then we kissed! . . . and we held . . . and we held . . .
the only thing moving, that usual propel,
till a small voice excused: Please would you budge up?
We budged up.

On the train I tore up my ticket for Tinos,
and greeted her cat in their chic little flat.
It lay on her bed and instantly purred
but left it outfaced by two loving lovebirds.

It's my parents I thank for the zeal of their love,
right from the start then fifty years on,
for I opened to Angelique right from the start
when our eyes clearly saw nowhere bars nor a lock
but a bright view, new sunlight, dispelling grey smog.

And we kiss still in public, we kiss all the time,
especially in France where it's highly approved.
In England it's frowned on like thick falling snow
but it's snow brought me luck and small talk in a queue
where a girl moved an easel so twenty years on
still the portraits I do with my hand of her face
say when love meets it travels to only one place.
And that place is beside her, just two in the queue,
going love-wards with ever,
chère Angelique,
tu.

Piers Browne

THE BOURBON ROCK LIGHTHOUSE CAPER

Late at night, while the lighthouse keeper sleeps,
his shadow dreams of moonlighting as a comic book hero . . .
but first it must escape the ever present menace
of the light beam in the guard tower above!

While the glaring spotlight looks the other way
The Shadow shimmies down the steep stone tower
to catch the Candy Island Ferry to the Bunny Hotel
where The Chiseller is waiting by a revolving door.

As The Shadow slowly pushes it forward
The Chiseller quickly moves to push it closed . . .
and the longest chase around the road to nowhere
begins in the main entrance of the Bunny Hotel.

Sparks fly as the door spins faster and then breaks
and the rivals fall in and a big foyer fight breaks out
and the crowd roar as The Chiseller is 'drowned'
by a vase wielding siren settling a score.

A cloud eclipses The Shadow's boxing prowess
and our story ends – with anti-climax! Epilogue-less
our story must end with the streets safe again . . . hang on!
The clouds part to reveal the dark heart of Middle Park
where The Shadow rescues a famous English explorer
who was grabbed by a lost tribe of indignant hobbits
when his light aircraft crash-landed in their forest.
Hooray!

Robert Black

THE HOT FRIDAY OF A LONDON JUNE

The train slows outside the station
Long enough to let me notice
Towering over the platforms' sleek arteries
A shard of glass and steel
Holding the sky in its nettle grasp
All around new tower blocks jostle
To London Bridge
The frantic pace of change
Echoed in the insistent alarm
And slow hiss of pneumatic doors
I alight into the hot Friday of a London June

First point of call is Southwark Cathedral
A quiet stay in the fabric of passing traffic
All welcome here, even the cat
And I marvel at the wooden bosses
The icon and the poet's tomb
I rub Will's knee for luck
And pause at the door
Visibly moved by the Marchioness Memorial
But the river runs on regardless

I walk with the quick pace of a city dweller
Not the slow doodle across the pavement
Of the day tripper who stops and stares
At every blue plaque and brass door-knocker
No, I sweep pass the Golden Hinde
And into Clink Street
A detour over Southwark Road
And Bankside finds me by the Globe
Neatly thatched and insular
To the passing street theatre
Clowns and mimes and Latin Americana

Now I am here
Outside the Tate Modern
Industrial cathedral
With it's hallowed spaces
Of art and culture held within
A red brick certainty

A coffee and biscuit on the members' terrace
As people wander over the Millennium Bridge
And sailing dinghies ply the stretch upriver
With a breeze as sharp as Cleopatra's needle

Down stairs and through doors
To find the Miro exhibition
In the theatre of his war
Every canvas his stage
Every print a soliloquy
To art
To freedom
Perhaps to dream
An infinite blue silence
Against the outrage
Of bloody oppression
No voice more eloquent
In these thronging rooms

On South Bank there's a beach
With sand and huts
And a large straw fox
It makes me laugh
The juxtaposition of this day
From surrealism to surreal
Sushi for lunch
Such a treat

Across the footbridge at Charing Cross
And on to Trafalgar Square
Where the sweet spray from the fountains
Cools the heat from my face
As light as summer rain
On the people's plinth sails a ship in a bottle
By the National Gallery a green wall grows
And here, the Olympic Clock, still ticking
Counting down my passing feet

Piccadilly and the Royal Academy
Sipping summer from room to room
As canvas after canvas adorn the walls
In ever greater scale and price
My eyes alight on beetled buttons
And a fat kingfisher
A dog rooting in a bin
A swirling red galaxy inexorably pulling me in
All punctuated by a circle and a square
The tide of fluorescent red dots
Rising up the wall
To remind me
The river runs on regardless

Now London in high afternoon heat
Heaps sweat and dust and noise on my brow
Rush hour soon as pavements swell
Under the bridge the neat rows of coloured lights
The final shattered bones of buildings
Being shored up with comedy clubs and beer cellars
And all around the commuters press ahead
To London Bridge

Against this human tide
I catch a glimpse
A face
A moment's recognition soon lost
They were heading in the other direction anyway
And my train is due

Patricia Herlihy

DRY RAIN

God's love rained down on us
But I put up an umbrella
And didn't see it or feel it.

We splashed in love filled puddles
But I wore my boots
And trod them at soul's length.

With my hat, coat, leggings and gloves
I protected myself and stayed dry
Until at home
I felt
Too dry
Too hot
Too dirty
So showered
but
stayed dry inside.

Chris Harbottle

I DREAM THE AIR OF YOU

Only in sleep
Will I relive the moments
Eyes wide shut and all I see
Is foreign coins
Hoping to buy a second
Of your time
Back
Into the next life
See I was never forewarned
The rules were meant to be broken
While eyes and hearts were simply stolen
Between dreams
Within blind moments
Of narcoleptic insomnia
A realisation in the shock
Of a woken sleep walk
And perhaps
In a single bubble
Of still watered thought
The absence of your breath
Into my atmosphere
Caused my mind to temporarily
Cease the need for oxygen
Now levitate
And hold that thought
In a hand clap of pavement cracks
And future fortunes
Hidden in the petals
Of concrete roses
Revealed by continuous small earthquakes
Creating a labyrinth
On the surface
Due to that
Lack of oxygen
And it would seem
I continue to need your air
To fuel my dreams

Joseph Baruwa

ABUSED

Girl racer, trying to grow up fast leaving the past.
I wanna know what it's like to be a woman.
I know I shouldn't.
To wear make-up and get my hair done.
To smoke, this ain't no joke.
I wanna be poked, in the night
with someone to hold me tight.
Someone who is not scared to show love.
I watch TV and see, women who have grown
and now know the love I want.
Can't you see, it's a plea to be free,
from a family who never loved me.
An abusing and using father
A mother who showed no love for another
A brother who's a junkie
and acts like a monkey
searching and cursing.
Never judge a book on how it looks
cos you could be mistook.
You don't know me or how I grew see.

I remember it well the hand that was dealt.
First happened when I was seven,
the mess that has brought me.
It started with a kiss in the dead of the night
I didn't fight, when he turned the lights on my youth.
See I was abused by my father
who refused to leave me to be young and free
He touched my body, when it wasn't mature,
and waged war on my emotions.
He gave me no potions to cure this misery.
I remember crying and feeling like dying,
each time the sun hid itself behind the moon.
Darkness brought this cancer into my life.
What is the cure?
Not my mother, she had too many lovers,
and couldn't discover that her daughter
was her husband's lover.
The pain went and came
I knew I would never be the same.
I lived with the excruciating pain.

As I got older, I became colder,
to everyone and everything
I hid myself in a fantasy world

of being someone else.
It helped me to conceal the sadness inside.
It was my secret and I would keep it,
to myself like everything else.
But now I'm 14 I see the damage he's done.
Do I listen to anyone? Especially not my mum.
I'm suffering in school, cos I'm not cool, to my peers
who give me stares, cos all the boys talk about me.
There is no doubt, they know I put out,
to the boys, that I think like me,
only to find, that they are not kind,
and cannot keep a secret, about me and them
and what we did and when.
The friends I have are what you would call 'bad'.
Their lives I expect have been like mine.
And time, has shown and unfolded the coldness,
that manifests into manic confusion.
Silence in words, our behaviour is that of a woman,
wanting the love of a man.
Our fathers taught us, that men have the power
to keep us under control, by using our bodies
to anchor their failings as men who can't satisfy real women.
Now we're suffering for them.
How do you feel?
You pig of a father, who took your daughter's virginity.
You showed no pity to your only daughter,
whose life has never be the same.
I'm twenty years old and still feel cold
when I think of how I was treated.
As said before a secret is a secret
I will keep all to myself.
Just tell myself it wasn't my fault.
He should have known better.
Forget about his reasons
They have no meaning to a life almost destroyed
Get some help for the wrong that I felt.
Move on and live my life.
Easier said then done it just
ain't no fun,
when you've lost all trust.

Maria Dyer

RICOCHET

The musty musk of office offal stench:
Dank desks and checkered chairs where backsides clench.
Those object organs oozing dirt and dust,
Incased in tessellating rooms of rust.

Bleak boardroom boredom: pinstriped streaks of strain.
Flat packed emotions unable to drain.
Square rooms restrain like skin the dark debris
And choke all thoughts of ever being free.

So clammy with the effort to repress
The feelings that he wanted her to guess,
He wrought them in to four sides in his head
Till all he saw was anger framed in red.

He told her she was duncy, ditsy, dumb:
Dumped wicked words and each one weighed a ton:
Hoped to hurt himself . . . but went to get her,
All because he wanted to feel better.

***

Through setting streets she swept the insults home;
Boxed carriages of crowds: commuter-drome.
Till kitchen tiles were weeping wet with steam
And one square meal was siphoned from her scream.

The kettle boiled the tension into cloud
And made her mention all her thoughts out-loud:
How he hardly ever even kissed her
Even though he called himself her mister.

He wasn't caring and it wasn't fair . . .
But squaring up to him to clear the air
She missed the target only passing on
The feelings that she wanted to be gone.

With viscous, vengeful, vitriolic screech
She lashed and clashed and crashed her hate-hot speech.
Said he'd changed so much from since he met her . . .
Hitting out she hoped to feel much better.

***

Voices rose like venom turned to vapour . . .
Sentences of smoke entwine and taper . . .
Till tendrils twist around a tousled head
And wake a toddler tucked up in his bed.

All creased and crumpled at the close of day,
Scared in his shadowed sheets by the melee,
Not knowing how to cope with all the noise
Of shouting takes an outing to his toys.

And looking for a missing puzzle square,
He hears a heavy footstep on the stair,
Bright banging light is shafted in his face;
A spotlight on the scene of his disgrace.

Then came the words; a tangled, torrid, torrent;
A spew of sounds all calling him abhorrent.
Too young to even understand the crime:
Absconding from his bunk at such a time.

***

The door slammed shut and washed the walls with black.
Stark sudden silence after the attack,
Which wasn't meant for *him* – but to off-set *her*.
Now there was no way to make it better.

Sobbing salty, snotty streams of sad,
A pelting, melting mood of molten bad.
Bleak bedroom bedlam: sniffy streaks of strain,
Tight-packed emotions unable to drain.

His tides of tears trace back to the square root,
The flow of feelings fated to transmute.
Thus veering off the office offal grey,
The boardroom boredom's bound to ricochet . . .

Anna Cookson

IF I HAD TO DIE FOR YOU

(Written for Lindy Jane)

If to hold your hand is wrong, then I will hug you,
If to kiss your tender lips is not right, then I will not stop,
If I had to cry for you, then I would cry a river,
If to love you is wrong, then I don't wish to be right,
If tomorrow never comes, then I'll love you for all our todays,
If I had to die for you, then I'm already dead.

C F Pollard

FROM THE DEPTHS

The sun starts to shine
Clouds begin to disappear
Plant life flourishes.
A burst of colours and growth
From the cold depths of winter.

John Stewart

REVENGE

'Come in Mrs Stockford, take a seat.'
I sit down and look at my feet.
Stomach churning, tears in eyes.
Knowing that this was my demise

Head pounding, my heart pumped.
A banging on the door, I jumped.
Policeman entered, stood by door.
I face two detectives mind in uproar.

It started the questions, I had expected.
So ferocious, that my mind was affected.
'Have you seen this before?' A knife?
'It was used to take your husband's life.'

I'm screaming inside but outwardly calm.
Trying to remember that day, at the farm.
I've got the bread knife in my hand.
I see red, 'Who is she?' I demand.

I'm actually saying, 'Who is she?'
Detective goes down on one knee.
Cuffs my hands, they drag me out.
I'm at home, been dreaming no doubt.

Cup of tea? No something stronger.
Must go see, can't wait any longer.
The whisky is soothing my nerves.
He's cheated, got what he deserves.

The kitchen is covered in blood.
On my knees, tears making a flood.
He croaks, 'Please call the police.'
I pick up knife, plunge, he's at peace.

Josie Stockford

SEASONAL SCENTS

The scent of spring is fresh and new,
It's primrose yellow and eggshell blue,
It's light and bright, it's clear and clean,
It's citrus sharp, it's young leaf green.
The scent of summer is strong and red,
The old earthy smell of the potting shed,
A full blown fragrance, all of its own,
Hot and heady, and garden grown.
The smell of autumn is gold and yellow,
It's rich and ripe, it's misty and mellow,
It's bonfire smoke and pungent hops,
The rural scent of harvest crops.
The scent of winter is cold and white,
It's cut glass sharp and brittle bright.
The smell of rain, of sleet and snow,
Of Christmas spice, and fireside glow.

Catherine Robinson

THE TORBAY SCENE

This tiny part of Devon set close by the sea
A wonderland of beauty its always been for me
At night when stars are shining I stand upon the shore
And gazing at it lovingly could ask for nothing more.
The velvet of the water reflects the coloured lights
Like ropes of beads in every hue a necklace for Dame Night.

Along her shore in sunlight the children laugh and play
Their bodies brown and healthy in costumes bright and gay
The buildings set among her cliffs the sea birds plumed in white
And red sands of her cliffs and coves all make a wondrous sight.
Flower beds with shrubs and plants exotic and perfumed
Ablaze with richest colours she offers up for you.

High above the Rock walk looking down on sea of blue
One thinks it is the South Seas for we boast of palm trees too
Some days when dark clouds gather the sea turns sombre grey
Waves begin to rear and leap like horses made of spray
I've watched my lovely Torbay in all her changing moods
From spring right through to autumn and even winter too
Always she will call to me no matter where I roam
Always and forever for me Torquay means home.

Dorothy Leech

THE WANTING

I went for a walk
and found my inner self
hiding up a tree,
hiding in a cuckoo's nest,
hiding from me.
She was all bruises,
her tongue gone,
her eyes wide with terror
and wild.

She fell into my arms.
I carried her up from the forest.
I kissed her beautiful little forehead.
I fed her honey and milk
and left her to sleep by the fire,
bathed in a duvet and dreams.

It got dark and I stayed,
awake until dawn,
staring at a silver screen.
I didn't mean to let it get so far out of hand,
but she's bigger
and stronger
and more me
than I could ever pretend to be.

I am a cuckoo,
broken out of the egg
into someone else's nest.

But what happens when all these grand ideas are seen for what they are?
I am just a dot to dot,
gone awry.
The older I get,
the littler I feel
and the more it seems that
the lines of my body are shrinking,
growing blurry,
shaking.
And parts of me are spilling
out into the air
drifting up,
into the atmosphere,
dissolving,
into blue nothing.

Never to be reclaimed by me:
a colour by numbers
fading slowly
to 8 bit greyscale.

Roseanna Dunlavey

IF I COULD ONLY HATE YOU

If I could only hate you;
I would hate myself a lot less.
If your voice scraped rusty
the canals of my ears
and aggravated my synapses
I would be able to bear you a lot more.
If I could only hate you so
my voice didn't tremble with fear each time we spoke
but you trembled in fear because of the hate
that you would sense I held for you,
I wouldn't verbalise as much fodder.
If only you could hate me too,
then I could hate you with ease,
and maybe our mutual hatred would become the spark
for some primitive carnal desire and we could
hate the clothes off one another's backs;
We could hate the sweat off each other's brows;
We could breathe heavy hate down our necks.
We could hate each other into screaming ecstasy
and whisper hatred to the pillow when falling asleep.
And when one of us wakes up we'll look at the other
with adoring hate glazing our eyes.
If only I knew how to hate you.

Josh Tuesley

TIMES ARE HARD

Life is superb
Of this we are sure
Times will get hard
But we shrug it to the floor

Money will be scarce
Good humour will slack
Times still are hard
It weighs down on our backs

Job Centre is King
With no end in sight
The recession a tyrant
With a heart black as night

Tempers will rise
As the black tyrant thrives
Pushing us down
Out of reach of his crown

Remember this friend
For when this time ends
You may cling to a shard
Of when times were hard

Charley Cox

ALMOST

It never began.

An ending to a solitary existence,
Was postponed by passive resistance.

Premature anticipation for something more,
Searching for somebody to adore.

Infatuation suggested your boundless potential,
This outcome shows how I was inconsequential.

Your words were of righteous indignation,
Denial told me they were lost in translation.

Tired of waiting for your consideration,
We stalled into desolation.

So it was over before it began.

Charlotte Harrison

WHERE LOVE GOES

The lady in the corner shop
Whose eyes twinkle as she adds a sherbet bomb
To the bag of penny sweets
Clutched in my little hand

The woman at the playground
Pushing her golden-curled baby on the swing
Laughing at his cherubic chortles
Smiling sadly at my haunted stare

The swan on the stage
Impossibly graceful; exquisitely beautiful
Twirling on tippy-toes
Pirouetting before this ugly duckling

The pretty lady in the photo
Cradling baby me
Loving baby me
Leaving baby me

She is everywhere I look
She is nowhere I look
She is all around
She is never found

A world full of mothers
But none is my own

One day, strolling in a park,
I will find her
In the rainbow cast by a fountain
In the fluttering in my womb

But now, age five
Pigtails askew
I am too young to know
Where Love goes

Charlie Wilson

AN INVASION OF PRIVACY

Beneath the ancient cedars on the corner,
And sheltered by a roof of shattered slate,
I suffer from a moment's hesitation
as I slice the frozen air, and my hand hovers at the gate.
The slightest push inflicts a shriek of protest,
The softest touch: a low, heart-wrenching moan.
But in ignorance I shove a little harder,
and it swings on rusted hinges over slabs of moss and stone.

Wading through neglected growth, so silently:
A ghost in someone's haunted memories.
Avoiding all the cracks and imperfections,
till I reach the peeling 'Welcome' sign, still creaking in the breeze.
The portal to another life hides shyly,
Smothered by: Those secrets never told;
the lies of those whose feet have crossed the threshold;
and the eyes that, through the keyhole, saw the lives therein unfold.

The letterbox has long since fallen useless,
but these details still elude the common man,
For a month's supply of letters line the hallway,
And I wonder how this spiral into disrepair began . . .
A biting, searing tingle rushes through me,
though I think it's more than just the winter's chill.
I'm sure this sad, dejected shack is empty . . .
But perhaps the person living here, is hiding in there still.

Too scared to leave the safety of their bedroom:
Their only home: their self-despising hell.
A skeleton just rattling round their graveyard:
Believing so completely that their past is buried well.
I glance down at the paper in my mitten:
'The Sun' with 'Brownies' Fun Day' on page two.
And I wonder if their vibrant, shining faces
could bring some fun and joy to this forgotten prison, too.

I lift my leaden mitten slowly, shyly:
My pitiful donation to such woe.
The smiles become a farce, a grim rehearsal.
The colours deaden slightly as my fingers let it go.
I feel the soft reluctance as it flutters.
I hear the resignation as it lands.
And I know I haven't even scratched the surface,
and that all that's ever left will be the ink stains on my hands.

Sarah Parker

I'M STUCK IN BETWEEN THESE FEELINGS

I'm stuck in between these feelings,
Of sorrow and confusion,
The covers of my bed,
Being only hug I can find,
The arguments in my head,
Too loud for sleep

I'm stuck in between these feelings,
Of hope,
Blowing boundless amounts of kisses to magpies,
Counting clouds in the sky,
Fixated on four-leaved clovers,
These little 'insignificant' moments are what keep me holding on,

I'm stuck in between these feelings,
Of being a child again,
Where being hyper was a daily routine,
Not old enough to understand,
Not old enough to remember,
But now old enough to drink to forget

I'm stuck in between these feelings,
Of where I belong,
Talking aloud,
To myself,
Pretending I'm on the phone,
The only way to blend into reality

I'm stuck in between these feelings,
Of wavering emotion,
The pain exacerbating as I try and lock it away,
Mutating into fire,
Extinguished,
By the teardrops that escape

I'm stuck in between these feelings,
Of life and death,
Not wanting love ones to be snatched,
From me,
These diseases engulfing,
Every piece of my heart

Samantha Howse

MY LONDON

This place right here. This street I'm walkin' on.
This fly infested trash, this slowly rotting man-made corpse.
This is where I call home. Where I belong.
And is this wrong? Well –

Let's wander through Wood Green, this crying street,
To Turnpike Lane, where a Kurdish man was shot a day ago.
And as we walk, in every face you'll see,
Marks of distrust, signs of feeling
low.
You'll notice groups of yutes just dossin' round.
No awareness of what's beyond these streets.
Everyone 'round here, they walk in packs.
Your local zoo, where endangered animals can be found.
This –
is where kids come after school to meet.

The Crude, the Bad and the Ugly.
Like proud dictators they prey,
On the desperate, sad and the struggling.
Bullied into fear, there isn't much they can say.
I ain't shocked 'bout that guy being shot the other day.
And na I ain't tryna look all hard by saying so,
it's just that I know.
That's what happens in a place where scum and drug lords come out to play.
The Turkish Kurdish community's dominant here.
But community. What community?
Look at this place. It's a state!
All people wanna cause each other is fear.
When you see me and my boys hangin' 'round the bookies.
Already you can envision our fates.
I swear yeah, in just about a year, five bookies have opened up.
Money, money, money, it rules us and our minds.
The more time you spend here, the less you believe in luck.
You see people don't realise. It's not just money they're bettin' with.
It's their lives.
Now the Olympics are coming up.
The countries hyped up. Seeing through rose tinted glasses.
But is transforming *one* run down area for the sake of public display enough? Coz I can still see loads of people out on the streets.
But not enough houses.
Actually forget about the houses.
It's not even about the houses. Would be better if it were.
Coz you see 'round here even the people with
houses are out beggin' on the streets.

You've got your:
Everyday drunkies
Women with young children
Constantly sleeping babies
Someone missing an arm
Someone missing a leg
Everyone's missing their hearts, no one using their heads.
Romanian child beggars.
You'd think someone would care.
A middle-aged woman. Mutton dressed as lamb,
stands on the street corner offering mindless men
Sour tasting treats.

But you all go ahead and build your fancy buildings.
It's all about pride. Hide the shame.
Sweep all that's ugly underneath shiny Westfield Shopping Centres.
As long as no one clocks on, no ones to blame.

But what about My London?
What do you know about My London?
Who's gonna transform My London?
Boris? Clegg? Mr Cameron?

No lies, just the other day, right here on this street.
I saw this little boy, only eight, at the bus stop, crying.
It was late and cold. Man he was only a kid.
I noticed him tremblin', and the those worn out trainers on his feet.
He said 'My dad's a little high. High and drunk.
I didn't wanna get hit. I came here,
so he couldn't find me.'

Welcome to our concrete jungle! Welcome to our place of Worship!
Welcome to the land of Injustice and Negligence. Welcome welcome!
Bienvenue, hoşgeldiniz. Sit down, take a seat,
take a stand where you may.
Ladies and Gents, Boys and Girls, Pimps and Hoes!
Yo! That spot where you're standing is where a dead
man once lay.
The history of our home should not be overlooked.
Erm . . . we've got gang crime, trafficking, prostitution, organ mafias, religious radicalism.
There's more than a few backstreet brothels 'round here . . . Hush-hush!
Each one overbooked.
Ten ten ten twenties and them fifties bitch!
Crack City.
Infamous pimps walk around with no hesitation.
The frustration.
And all of this degradation is glorified and persuaded
into the young people's minds and vision.
The block of flats my grandma lives in overlooks

The breathtaking view of Wood Green's back streets.
Home to many families. Kids are out all day long.
Playing, laughing, smoking, smashin', crying. The joys of childhood.
Grow up to be a big man. Never admit defeat.
Up on the balcony I feel like a hopeless God,
witnessing it all. My kingdom's fall.
One day you'll see someone come hide a shank in
the rubbish bins. The next day, someone's dying,
someone's hiding. And all of us . . . We're lying.

This place right here. This street I'm walkin' on.
This fly infested trash, this slowly rotting man-made corpse.
This is where I call home. Where I belong.

Meral Duzgun

JUBILEE

I found a photograph today.
No red, white or blue, just grey.
A trestle table filled the tiny street,
Loaded with marvellous things to eat,
Unknown until the end of rationing.
Grandma, her tiny figure hunched under her dusty, rusty, black felt hat,
Smiled with her puckered, limp-lipped mouth.
A baby on her knee, my elder sister Pat
Took pride of place.
Between the two there peeped a face,
Hair awry, teeth missing, cheeky but shy.
Why, yes it's I!

It was to welcome our new Queen.
Whom no one there had ever seen
Those sixty years ago.
For us there was no telly then.
We couldn't watch the splendour when
She drove up to be crowned.
Time has moved on.
I'm here but some of them are gone.
And now at Jubilee the nation shares in coloured pageantry and show.
Yet in my mind I felt somehow
Much nearer to my Queen than now.

Kezia Howells

MIRROR, MIRROR ON THE WALL

Is this a willow tree I see?
A harsh array of shrubbery
Beneath a frozen bark of steel.
Amidst the naked branches
The eerie frozen eyes of an owl;
Distinguished in their blankness
And stillness at the wind.
This owl is not wise,
It sits and stares in the willow's disguise.

But what emerges in the image –
Can it be? The arms of porcelain
All dried, and cracked, and weak –
Too weak to create a muse from mud –
Too weak to even stir someone's heart.
The dust is descending on a rugged rug –
A rigid rugged rug of a soul in an undisturbed sleep.
Blood oranges thumping down the elongated stairs
Choking every opportunity for a gulp of air.

There is a fire in the forest –
And life is dying there.
Will it swallow the willow tree,
And will the dumbfounded owl stir?
It will most certainly burn out like a match;
It will not leave a trace of its existence.
I gaze at the willow tree and all I see
It is looking back at me,
Weeping silently.

Tatiana Aksarova

WHICH WAY TO WONDERLAND?

On bright afternoons as a boy I would sit at my grandmother's table
and draw Alice Liddell, child muse of Lewis Carroll,
as she appeared in his sweet, demented world.
Beneath her crude likeness I would tell Carroll's story
in my childish tongue, again and again, on paper left
by my great-grandfather (his will would leave me reams of it).

Sat in a world of blank and flawless logic,
a machine performing simple tasks, which can't be argued with
or changed, Wonderland appealed to me.
Beside me were large windows which received the sun
like water through a hole in a ship. The room was always capsizing.

Jack Heslop

COVERED

Young Frank and Tony, it is plain
Hated playing in the rain
To the fireside they retired
Whilst damper children never tired

Although the wet kids thought them freaks
Some saw them more as useful geeks
On numbers, records, sporting stats
They're both as sound as cricket bats

Their lonely childhoods long complete
The dusty duo chanced to meet
They hit it off, like, straightaway
And soon knew where their future lay

Like G and T, or pint and pie
Their partnerships will never die
Whilst cricket's played, and clouds are black
Their system we will never lack

Like war, a rained-off match is hell
But now we have our D and L
A fair result at last now due is
Courtesy of Duckworth/Lewis

Chris Barton

UNCERTAINTY

The feeling of content quickly sweeps away,
As my brain begins a new day,
What's the problem now I say?
Insecurities? Unemployment? Sexism?
Choose one quickly,
Feeling lost is always your forte.

Yes, lost! It's that feeling again!
'You feel that a lot?' says a friend,
'Only very rarely' I pretend,
Can't let them think I'm too mental.

So what is the problem exactly?
I'm unsure what is expected of me,
Just be yourself it's that easy,
I really wish it was.

I'm a young, female graduate and I'm frightened,
In a life where my opportunities should be widened,
But at this time I lack faith in the supposed enlightened ,
As I read certain things.

I'm struggling to find a job position,
Experience is my only recognition,
Many are thrown my way but there's always one condition,
It is once again unpaid.

I feel this is not my only problem,
Sometimes I struggle to be a young woman,
Expectations and stereotypes I still cannot fathom,
But I'm anxious to complain.

I've become enraged by sexist opinions and remarks,
But scared of the reaction my response will spark,
'Here we go with that feminist lark'
'I'm not a feminist but . . . ' I shamefully say.

When will I be happy within my own company?
When will I sit alone and not think so glumly?
What's the problem now I say?
Insecurities? Unemployment? Sexism?
Choose one quickly,
Depression is always your forte.

Toni Toms

WHAT DO YOU SEE?

When you to look in the mirror what do you see? Do you see someone that is pure and naïve or knowledgeable, treading down that cold, dark path in that journey of independence, crunching on the leaves of mistakes?
Do you see someone that is beautiful or ugly, as the insecurities wrap around you like a cocoon as your chest closes in?
As the hours inevitably melt away, does your story lie ahead or does your face tell a story, fading away like a water-colour painting as the paint brushes resemble embarrassment or pain? When you see strangers passing by, do you simply exchange an infectious smile or walk on by, injecting people with stony discontent?
When memories flood back to you, do they fill you with happiness or drown you with sorrow, anchoring your heart to the inside of your body and slowly feeling it sink to the bottom?
Thinking back to the furthest memory, does it make you wise or old, being forgotten, as the newest generation do not understand and accept your information?
When you feel, do you enjoy watching the rain from inside or do you mourn at the damp unpleasant sky, feeling surpressed and saddened, as the spell of pathetic fallacy takes over?
When you are lost, are you guided or do you feel lost, that there's no one directing you back to safety, shining a light on your track?
As you to look in the mirror you should see a knowledgeable person who has stepped out of that tunnel of learnt mistakes, allowing the stream of purity flowing through your veins, and honour being the light seeping out at the end of the tunnel.
That cocoon which coils around your ugly body produces a colourful, delicate and beautiful butterfly, floating through the sky, sophisticated and wondrous; the most unpleasant of things have greatness about them.
As the hours inevitably melt away, the canvas becomes a masterpiece, creating a vast audience as more art is added to the canvas; it earns the proud integrity of the one that once hid behind the story.
As the strangers pass by, the smiles pass on, making their hearts fill with joy as your mouth has caused one simple action, as if it was like handing out leaflets.
As the memories flood back, think about the happy recollections, allowing you to feel relaxed and care free as though you were calmly sailing into the beautiful and peaceful sunset.
As you think back to the furthest memory, know it makes you wise; as you look into the mirror and study your face, know it makes you an interesting and beautiful person. Your wrinkles determine your labour and existence and your soulful and wise eyes show a story, like a historic book.
As you feel, stepping outside and feeling the light raindrops is an intrepid and new opportunity to embrace; the rainbow is the pathetic fallacy, reflecting the bright and happy sensation, feeling free and contented, noticed and picturesque.
As you feel lost, that gut feeling will be your guidance, your mother, father and guardians will have taught you well for you to know that your own compass is your heart.
You will always see things differently,
But could you see yourself differently?

Sophie Dallaway

21ST CENTURY SUMMER IDYLL?

Leather on willow, bat on ball
Summer sun shining upon us all
The village green with its verdant hue
A cloudless sky boasting an azure blue

This is the image we portray
When in reality the sky is grey
Three sweaters protecting us from the cold
It is not the vision we've been sold.

The 'chocolate box' reverie is no more
Grudges are held and the bile doth pour
It's uncivil war out at the wicket
A far cry from owt to do with cricket

'LBW? Come on Ump!
That ball was flying past leg stump.'
He trudges off – his head is bowed
Venting his scorn at the baying crowd

Nurturing long held feuds on the field of play
Helps to pass the time away
At least until lunch when they get fed
With Spam, corned beef and 'value' bread

Insipid tea, limp sarnies, dry cakes
That's what the amateur 'Delia' makes
There's a lack of interest in the modern day
Just turn up with whites and you can play.

Don't kid yourself
'Twas ever thus

S W Brade

EPISOZOMENE

A wish breathes, wording streamed by waters
My bodily senses awaken
Heaven's electricity alters
Muscles-sparking, restlessness taken

Wonderful wash, episozomene!
This imaginable happening
Perfusion affecting bone and gene
Listen to my strangled voices sing!

Gifts from God, I long to be near you
Running as blessings thrive through the years
Winds attack the stone of heartaches blue
Eons of joy, remembrance dries tears

Stephen Wren

UNTITLED

To hold a dream and make it real.
To hold a heart in whispered breath.
A love held fast, by sweet caress.

Weave your future, truly blessed.
Of happy smiles and woes redressed.
Bear no grudge, hold not tight regret.

Take what life throws at you by the hand.
Mix it, meld it in your plan, enjoy.
Love, death, births, in tapestry employ.

To hold a dream and make it real.
To hold a heart in whispered breath.
A love held fast, by sweet caress.

Angela Gould

ROSE'S BEFALLEN

Awakened dreams, nightmarish quips
Jaundiced tear drops, blooded thrips

Winter's sloe in wrathful mourn
Howled wails of petalled thorn

Fingers touch, perusing caress
Sombrous smile, blackened fluoresce

I will seek her out, birth unto passing
Hearts yearning for florets final classing

Our time maybe up, admonition finally waned
Our hearts will now soar; soulless, coupled feigned.

When the leaves fall and the soul hath turned grey
Her smile will guide me, world's alluring soiree

Chaining wrists in fearful descent
Battered seething, tearful lament

Whispering tales of eerie virtue
Blooded trails in vengeful curfew

Divinity's penance, extricating excursion
Virulent essence, fornicating perversion

Every time I hope, reverie's clasped away
Feeling my heart bleed, weeping, rendered flay

Advent your love, resplendent, so sprue
You wish me away, obdurate, in strew

I thought we would fleet towards the stars
I have been left with tears, rupture and scars

You bid me farewell
Longing resolve in couple,
Heart's fragmented,
Pollen now supple . . .

What to define? Silent words unspoken
The Hellish vine, embracing fragment's broken

May the most you wish for, be the least you get
Expect the unsurprising addition of now's not yet

Benjamin David

A PROPHETIC REVELATION OF AN UNRIGHTEOUS WORLD

I was born in its beauty and walked in its paths,
Guide me with confidence it seemed to have been;
In relaxation and excitement I became comfortable,
Only to tumble down and heard it laughing

Through my dreams and hope I gained courage
And on my feet I stood up,
I thought I had its security and aimed higher
Only to stumble and heard it laughing

Loosing hope was never my faintness,
Stood up for another path I did,
Believing in better kept me expecting
In my mind's thoughts I visualised the winning line
Only to be blinded and heard it laughing

With exhaustion and disheartened I asked myself
Why when I understand they cheat me,
When I trust them I gain lies,
When I love them they deceive me;
Moreover laughing is what they couldn't stop!

Asking myself in faith for an answer;
I gazed upon the realm unseen,
What is this place?
Only to know this is where I am;
A place never to make home
An unrighteous world

Seer Blessing Munashe Makande

WOUNDS OF LOVE

You, like me, have discovered how painful it can be to care for another.
Be it a friend, lover or a brother.
To care you must be willing to be hurt
By those who you consider to be your kith and kin.
This knowledge doesn't help when the pain sets in.
The wounds of your loved one are your wounds too.
Sometimes there is nothing you can do
Until your loved one wants to heal their wounds too.

Lorna Smart

AS I WAIT . . .

I sit
I stare
I cry
As I watch everything around me,
People screaming and shouting,
As slowly families are dying.

I stand
I'm shocked
I weep
There's a shout, a loud cry,
People running, stumbling,
As a house rips up in flames.

I huddle
In the corner
Scared to death
I hear the guns being fired,
The bombs dropping down,
The ground shaking like an everlasting earthquake.

I look around
Skies black
Roads red
The streets are an open cemetery,
The houses are a living hell,
The people are the walking dead.

I sigh
As I wait
And I pray
For the day I can smile again,
When the skies will be free from sin,
When the day the war comes to an end.

Fahmida Variava

JUST US 2

How can I express in so many words
The feelings in my heart your presence has stirred
I want you to feel the beat of my heart
Before I embrace you and we'll never part

Can you see how you cause me to act
The fool or a clown could never distract
You're my centre of being, my own galaxy
I'm constantly surprised that you only want me

These feelings are real and straight from my soul
You're just like a whirlpool that's swallowed me whole
I'm caught in your web of intimacy
You're pulling me toward you with mere gravity

I constantly crave the touch of your skin
You're perfection without measure, not that I could begin
I don't have to dream any longer of you
You're always beside me in all that I do

The only person that I can't hide from is you
But why should I try when I have no need to
I'm higher than sky and brighter than stars
You heal my pain and soothe all my scars

The wait is now over and the day will be soon
But unlike a flower my love is always in bloom
With you always beside me there's nothing I can't do
'Cause there isn't just two ones anymore

For now there's just us 2.

Adrian Horton

I TALK TO MY BANANA

I talk to my banana, Daddy says I'm mad.
I talk to my banana, why is that so bad?
Banana was so happy growing on a tree.
But now the poor banana will be lunch for me.
When banana was little he'd have thoughts of his own
He'd not expect to be my lunch when he was fully grown.
I 'spect banana's feeling sad, a long way from home
And missing his mum and dad, out here on his own.
I talk to him to calm him, I think that he is scared.
I know he cannot talk back, but he will know I cared.
But Daddy says bananas feel no pain or joy
And they cannot talk at all unlike a small boy.
As bananas cannot talk, there was no way a bunch
Was able to tell Daddy they'd hate to be his lunch.
Daddy's getting old and grey, he's nearly thirty three.
I bet when he was little he had pet fruit like me.
Daddy says I'm far too big to treat my fruit like toys.
Daddy says that things like that are just for little boys
Daddy isn't fair to me, isn't fair at all.
When I want what big boys have, Dad says I'm too small.
Daddy talks to lots of things when on marijuana
So why is it wrong for me to talk to my banana?
Jenny gives names to her dolls, they give her great delight.
She talks to them at bedtime; she kisses them goodnight,
She dresses them in bedclothes, pretty pink pyjamas.
But they have never been alive, unlike my bananas.
I do love my banana, but can't talk to it now.
Because my poor banana – I've eaten it somehow.

John Alec Shepherd

EXPLICIT

The sky is falling with silver stars tonight
Every sound different from either waves
Bloodstained hair whips at my peeling skin, as my feet stand upon crushed leaves
An acid taste fuels my mouth ,during the white months
A burning from within drives my desire to the darkness
After all these years of eternal slumber, again you awaken
The blueness of the ocean now darkened by your cloak
Everywhere I travel you are never far behind
I can feel your breath on my neck
I can almost remember the taste of you
So bitter yet still I find myself craving you once more

Dylan Halliwell

MY PAINTING ON THE WALL

Upon the wall my painting stares at me;
I wonder if it also stares at thee?
It shows to me that time and patience pays,
But burns and fades in light of window rays.
The sun, my love, it only counts our time;
Each rise and fall, each uninspired rhyme.
The colour runs and slowly fades away,
Akin to sun and moon at wane of day.
The seasons, aye, a common theme of death;
Winter akin to autumn's final breath.
Alike to me, my painting on the wall,
Of seasons gone, of days ere yet to fall.
I'll watch it till my eyes can watch no more;
When both are burnt and gone for evermore.

Amanda Killington

FAIRIES

The beating of wings
Little voices sing
In snow rain and sleet
The patter of tiny feet
They hide in woods, lakes and streams
Some are kind some are mean
They all live in the imagination of dreamers

Stephen Frederick Black

CAMPING IN WALES

The trees gathered around our field in crowds
Sceptical spectators, watching and waiting
How long would we stay? Would we survive?
Trespassers of solitude and wild countryside

Rain followed rain, hitting our canvas
A continuous stream of random gunfire
Still we remained, solid adventurers
Refusing to move, tough till the end

Along came the wind, wild fast and furious
Searching for gaps to whip, whizz and fly
Through our clothes, our tent, our belongings
Seeking a path in destructive delight

Saturated and soggy we sat in our dampness
Petal pink cheeks under thick woolly hats
Heavily stained, bright red moustaches
Heinz tomato soup, drunk from a flask

Sticky and chewy Robinsons Malt loaf
Cloggy and heavy but oh what a feast
We will not leave, we will not be defeated
For Camping in Wales is a delight not a feat

Sara Wood-Emery

THE BALLAD OF JUANNA THE MAD - FIRST QUEEN OF SPAIN

(This poem was inspired by a real character from history, I think her story has an left an echo that can still be heard today.)

There was a queen and it was said,
That she was manic – wrong in the head.
Her name Juanna and queen of Castile,
And, with her life she could not deal.
To Philip the handsome she was wed,
Six children came from the marital bed.
In the fourteen hundreds did Juanna live,
To be a queen her life did give.

Oh Juanna so very mad were you,
Oh Juanna the best that they could do.
Was to lock you up away from the day,
But that was for your safety oh say they say.
Perhaps they were right we will never know,
But Juanna you still cause so much woe.

Philip with Juanna was, just for her throne,
And soon, her life was not her own.
He cheated on her again and again,
And this would help to send her insane.
So of the plague now Philip died,
And very few tears Juanna cried.
But of his body she would not let go
Because the crown she wanted so.

Oh Juanna so very mad were you,
Oh Juanna the best that they could do.
Was to lock you up away from the day,
But that was for your safety oh say they say.
Perhaps they were right we will never know,
But Juanna you still cause so much woe.

And so Juanna they locked away,
In a convent to keep mad at bay.
For fifty years she lived all alone,
While others had her life and throne.
And so she died locked up insane
But people write of her again and again.
Would they now find her quite so mad?
Or just depressed and really sad?

Oh Juanna so very mad were you,
Oh Juanna the best that they could do.
Was to lock you up away from the day, But that was for your safety oh say they say.
Perhaps they were right we will never know,
But Juanna you still cause so much woe.

And to the Juanna's of today,
Be careful of the games you play.
Don't mess with people's dreams and fears,
Or you could end locked up for years.

Victoria Bartlett

THE ABC OF A DISHONEST MAN

Able-minded and strong at heart
Bravely hiding all insecurities
Could this be a ruse?
Devoid of any true emotion
Every now and then,
Feint glimpses into the inner self
Grave misconceptions
Hover over the spray-on persona
Instigating ingenuity beyond expectation
Jaded smiles conceal a quivering lip
Killing the urges to reveal the lies
Losing yourself in your own manipulations
Mutilated aspirations
Never reaching the potential you set
Ousted by social constraints
Pending logic as reason hibernates
Quietly wishing to return back to your past
Reversing the disease you proudly created
Still, hope lingers should you choose to change
Tender emotions within a fragile core
Undo the curse and shed the tears
Verily the veils can be removed
Willpower left to be desired
Xenobiotic traits slain to vanquish infection
Yesterday's cruel past now taught as history
Zen is restored

Noor Alhadi

THE OAK AND THE MAN

Here stands this great and mighty oak
Its roots twisted, deep, held firm beneath the scree,
The hillside ground enlisting.
Upon this mound, amid the skies, grows the mighty tree,
Its branches broad and spreading, like a cloak,
All weathers still resisting.

Like silent sentinel it guards the vale,
Weathered, knotted, full of burr
It grips the steep incline.
Through storm winds, gales, snow and hail
Surviving all that does occur,
It stands, a testament to age and time.

Beneath its wide and welcome awning,
Below its strong and spreading boughs,
Surrounded by its shades.
There sits an aged man at early morning,
Whose memory long his mind invades,
And loses track of time and days.

He sits with back against the hollowed trunk,
His body melded to its form,
And seeks to make amends.
He has a sad and gentle story,
Of friendship lost, asunder torn,
To tell within the old oak's glory.

He has a tale that will be told,
He has a story that will unfold.
Of happy days, of fields and ways,
Of past delights and halcyon days.
Of endings sad, of jubilation
Of happiness and lamentation.

Let's listen now before the breath of hoary ages,
Breathes its last and leaves our pages.
Let's listen now while life is strong,
Before the heart gives out ere long.
Let's listen now to tales of past,
Before our old man breathes his last.

Let's give ear to wind and land and song,
Let's join the memories of pasts that throng,
Amidst the valley along the lane,
Accompanied by joy, regret, sorrow and pain.
Let's listen now one and all alike,

Before the enemy death does strike.

Come now with me a journey make,
Through labyrinth of mind and hearts.
Come now with me and secrets see,
Entombed within the hidden parts.
Come now with me your vision take,
Beneath this old and battered tree.

Peter Hewett

SIXPENCE NONSENSE

Down the drain
Went my pound
But I tripped on a sixpence
In the ground

I'd found a penny
And lost a note
I was an
Unfortunate bloke

The time it had
Reached a quarter past one
I drank my tea
And had a current bun

The sun was out
And I would spend
My sixpence on
My best friend

His name was Davie
He had a car
We used to drive
To Wallmart

But today we were skint
So we bought a chew

Thomas Latcham

SNOW WHITE

There was a mirror with magic powers,
Into which the Queen would stare for hours
And upon each day she would cry
Into this mirror that did not lie
'Mirror, mirror on the wall
Who is the fairest of them all?'
To which each day it did respond
'Why you of course you bombshell blonde.'
Until upon one summer's day,
Much to the wicked Queen's dismay,
The mirror it did change its tone
When it said 'The heiress to the throne.
Snow White's beauty but does grow more
White skin, red lips and a body to die for.
I'm afraid dear Queen, if truth be told
Next to her you look quite old.'
At this the Queen flew into a rage
And could not speak for many days.
Eventually she began to mutter
'Someone please, bring me the woodcutter.'
She commanded that in the dead of night
He was to knock off poor Snow White.
To bring her heart upon a plate
And do it by tomorrow's date.
So that very night in Snow White's room
The woodcutter he crept right through the gloom
But upon his movement she did rise
And opened up her emerald eyes.
By her beauty he was won
And the wicked Queen's plan was overcome.
I must let her live, he did think.
Then proceed to ask her for a drink,
But before he could pursue that date
Snow White, was out the palace gate!
Into the woods and over the hill
She ran so far and further still.
Until she stumbled on a house
So small it could be for a mouse!
From the window through the glass
There was a cry of 'Here at last!'
For seven little merry men
Each no taller than two foot ten,
Spied Snow White and began to think
There's washing up our kitchen sink,

There's clothes needing hanging out to dry,
She could reach the cobwebs way up high.
So with the dwarfs Snow White did stay
And cooked and cleaned and worked all day.
The dwarfs they worked her to the bone
But alas she stayed since she had no home.
Until one day the Queen found out
That Snow White was still about
But this time the Queen knew what to do.
She bought an apple red in hue
And in that apple she did hide
A lethal dose of cyanide.
That evening as the sun went down,
The little dwarfs began to frown.
As they felt great pain within their tummy
They thought their pie had been so yummy.
The dwarfs so fat and full of greed
Had gobbled up the pie with speed,
So poor Snow White was left with none,
Left sat in the kitchen till dinner was done
When she entered what a sight she saw
All seven dwarfs lying dead on the floor!
Since after eating that apple pie
Each dwarf began to die.
Another wicked plan undone
Away from the crime scene Snow White did run.
Back into the woods, back over the hill
She ran again so far and further still
To the home of that handsome chap
The woodcutter with his mighty axe.
So when one day the Queen did come
To see Snow White with a loaded gun
She had no time to take her shot
For Snow White devised a cunning plot!
Up she picked her husband's axe
And gave her stepmother a good few whacks.
Then their days were filled with love and laughter
Snow White and the Woodcutter, happily ever after.

Elizabeth Roberts

AN ABSENCE OF HUMANITY

Wonder me not and ponder me true
The hills remain still yet the river flows through
A dulcet voice echoes through newly lit skies
The call of the day as the rooster doth rise

Unlike verjuice the prospects are sweet
No garish imposters storm by their feet
Their supercilious smiles are nowhere to be seen
Just immaculate fields of yellows and green

A land where avarice has long been unknown
Benevolent teachings are all it has sown
The hubris nature of the humans can stay
In a distant land mass much further away

Zahra Al-Hadi

BLANK CANVAS

Come to me and I shall expose you;
For I know the truth when others see white.
Deceiving yourself will get you nowhere
Time to partake in this graphic fight.

With heavy strokes your bleeding commences
No self defence, accepting your fate.
Standing there silent as a solemn statue
As you transit to this coloured state.

Vibrant violets and verdant blotches;
Rouges and ambers reveal your lies!
No more returning to your innocent past-
The picture formed will sever those ties.

It's true I've exposed you; forever you shall be
Hanging in shame for all to see.
No point in crying or bluntly denying,
Your new persona has come to be.

Ayah Ameer

LAMENT

Rounds and rounds of lament
Going round and around without end
Wind and rain
The wind laments the rain
'Let me blow where I will
Your wetness is in my way
Your glistening pavements
Your pretty flowers – alive again
You are in my way!'

The rain laments the wind,
'Stop blowing me around
I'm going where I don't want to go
I am powerless in your hands
Let me do my work in peace
I won't always be here
I come and I go
I lament the wind that gets in my way!'

Do the dead lament their wasted lives?
Do they wish they had taken opportunities to use their gifts more than to earn a living?
Do they regret holding back their love because true love costs too much?
Do they wish they had grasped their loved ones to their chests and whispered 'I love you' gently in their ears?
Do they lament not smiling, not kissing on the cheek and saying, 'Thank you'?

Do the tears of the dead fall down on our heads when we lament it is raining!
Do the wistful wishes of the dead swirl around the gardens, fields and forests and mountains
Crying out, 'I wish I had shown you I loved you more'

I lament the wind and the rain
I lament your death
You have gone
I lament your passing from this life
But you did love me and you told me in so many ways

My lament is drowned out by the sound of the wind and rain
I welcome the wind and the rain
For every day of my life I can hear you singing
I can see you smiling
I can feel your heart beating
I know you are alive
You heal my pain
I am amazed I am alive
I am happy again

Maria Dabrowska

THE INVITATION

I got an invite yesterday,
an invitation very dumb.
It didn't say an awful lot.
In fact, it just said 'Come'.
'Come where,' I thought, 'and when and how,
and who would be the host,
and was it full scale haute cuisine
or only jam and toast?'

Just who would send a card like this
that said not where to go?
They must be mad if they assumed
I didn't need to know.

I put it down and went about
my normal daily life.
I didn't need a conundrum.
I didn't need no strife.
But then it struck me that this word
was all I need to know.
And all I need to do is trust
and let myself just go.

Where'er I go he will be there.
The food will be just right.
The timing's also optional
throughout the day or night.
One step is all it takes to meet
the everlasting Lord.
The invitation need consist
of just one single word – 'Come'.

Tim Nice

AUTUMN

I'm looking at a white marshmallow sky,
The background blues of various hues
Complete the scene.
This autumn day, so crisp and golden
Reminds me of my childhood,
When school began and overcoats and
Sensible shoes
Appeared for all
Heralding the climate change
From Summer to the Fall.
My favourite time of year.
When nights draw in and the scent of woodsmoke fills the air,
When fires in grates are lit, the glow illuminating dark
Corners of the room.
Then off to bed in dim dark rooms
Lit only by the clear, silver light of the moon,
Its blue white light, shimmering across the bed
Pointing you towards a life to come,
When to simple thoughts and scenes like these
You may never again succumb.

Gerry de Faoite

LIFE

Life gives you laughter, love, sorrow and pain,
Happiness, terror, hatred and fun.
Whatever life brings just try to gain.
Try to stay warm and bask in the sun,
Don't be cold-blooded, cold-hearted and mean.
Stay with true friends and they'll stay with you.
There are so many things to be seen.
Be inspired, creative, you can win too!
Care for others and cherish the world.
You may be successful, rich and have fame.
Just let your imagination become unfurled,
Don't be a bully because it's just lame!
Give to life everything you've got,
And life will give you back a lot!

Eleanor Evans

THE PERFECT CONTAINER

There live upon my epidermis
A host of very weeny germies.
They're not conspicuous on my surface.
If I could see them, I'd be nervous!
But I wonder if my colonies –
Devoid of any tiresome fleas –
Appreciate how precious to me
Is my packaging epitome?

Because I'm self-contained by an all-embracing, elasticated,
Dent resisting, shower-proofed and ventilated,
Super soft, cushion-backed and decorated,
easy clean and biodegradable *skin!*

Both front and back from top to toe
It tells me all I need to know.
And furthermore, though weather-beaten
It tells me when I'm overheating,
Or drawing pins are busy pricking
And splinters into fingers sticking,
And if I'm itching, stinging, clammy,
Or twitching, pimpled or just plain jammy.

Limp or smooth, powdered or scented,
It's the greatest container ever invented.
No better place to be inside
From baby's bottom to elephant hide.
Purest lotions and creams all ensure
My complexion lasts for evermore.
For burning bronze or ghastly white –
It will be moisturised tonight!

A tickle it will not ignore,
Or foreign body in a pore.
Who cares if hard or even callused –
Be thankful it will never rust!
This surface has a multifunction
Guarding the atmospheric junction.
It's virtues are much more than visual –
Never call my beauty superficial!

Because I'm self-contained by an all-embracing, elasticated,
Dent resisting, shower-proofed and ventilated,
Super soft, cushion-backed and decorated,
easy clean and biodegradable *skin!*

Laila Lacey

LOST GENERATION

As the blood begins to pool on a now claret stained street
A once heart of stone struggles then dies, it has taken its last beat
Life has now ebbed away and a young soul departs this world with its maker to meet
What has brought on this turn of events
Why is this a common site, what has led to this unholy precedence

Too many youths defending their corners, willing to pay the ultimate price
So many potentials lost with a bullet or a knife
No hope no dreams, just a grey drab imprisoned life
It's not just the lost souls in her majesty's prisons
Have a thought for the neglected ones who grow with no aspiration or vision

People say it's a lack of respect and discipline in school
But how can a teacher educate someone who wishes to play the fool
Where success counts for nothing, what's important is the cool
An environment where being the gangster is a desirable state
Britannia is sinking, we need to change course before it's too late

There is a way we can stop this violence plaguing our land
A positive message needs to be screamed, together we must stand
Reach out to the hopeless ones, give friendship offer a hand
Be a beacon of hope illuminating a more righteous path
Shine love like a torch, turn a frustrated scream into a laugh

If you say there is no hope for the youth
Then you must prepare yourself to accept an unthinkable truth
That your own future is hopeless, I offer this as a harsh proof
The generation you sit and write off today
Will be the generation that supports you when you're old and grey

So if you don't wish to resign yourself to a future that's bleak
Get up make a difference, bring love to the streets.

Luke Bowden

HUES OF SUMMER

Out in the sunshine on balconies
A perfect view of aqua sea,
One has red hearts, another shoes,
Turquoise dolphins with swirly pink hues!
Blue football teams, Caribbean dreams
Too hot pink and princess themes!
Others are stripy, some are bright
They deserve to be in hot sunlight.
There's *psychedelic* squares, others plain,
Another with Cacti and a plane.
There's a little Thomas the Tank Engine train . . .
A red and white Turkish flag - *in Spain!*
The lion king, a lizard thing -
A life jacket with a rubber ring!
Palm trees, bumblebees, coral seas,
Calm breeze, Florida Quays, golf tees!
Marijuana, plants of peace -
Orange sunsets - maps of Greece!
A turtle crawls on scorching sand
She must have been to many lands.
South Park and a plight for Kenny;
Hot hot playboy-there are so many!
Homer, Bart - a fright scream;
Purple sauce on yellow ice cream!
Dogs, cats, flip-flops, straw hats,
Frogs, bats, big spots, goofy rats!
Brighton Pier, a sandy beach,
A bottle of beer, some candy sweets.
Bright blue lions with lime green manes
But time has passed and once again
They sadly only seem to appear
Occasionally over the years,
Now folded away in cold dark drawers
Where memories of good times are stored.
Forgotten our beach towels tucked away,
Until they're used for our next holiday.

Linda Lawrence

WHEN WHAT ONCE WAS

O children,
If we could only go back again,
For I'd rather the joy of our play than this pain,
The small sticky hand in my hand in the rain,
And Lesley and snow and the puddle-filled lane.

The summery, dusty field was so wide
Where we noisily ran with the sun on our side,
And all of the ribbons of rules were untied
And Lesley was laughing for joy.

What strange irony can the riddle mean,
That the wonder of children can only be seen
With a backward glance but once it has gone,
Though all of the turning of days may go on . . .

Better it was with no cares to have run
Beneath the stretched arms of the very first sun,
Or when our shoes slapped the slush and our cold breath was seen,
And on the black gate at dusk
I with Lesley would lean.

Kevin Ryan

VISIBILITIES OF PURPOSE

Spark fire onto temples of might and thrones
And they would succumb to the frost of winter nights
Gods of unseen spirits can rage war in rebel,
But they cannot hold unto the untimely running of diarrhoea
A dungeon of hidden armoury can awake.
Vampires and witches can loiter for blood,
But they cannot stand the tears of the mid-day sun
Volcanoes and typhoons can sweep the earth,
But it cannot burn or wash the good in you
For we will not sacrifice our souls to throws of arrows
And clinches of swords due to hollow brawls
But rather,
Spare the deer from spears,
Just for that one word, 'Peace'.

Michael Kwaku Kesse

PAST LOVE

Wanting to let go of a past love
Through pain, desire, wanting and belonging
The wish to go back in time to fix the broken heart
The pain of realisation that nothing will bring it back
The love that made you once whole
The love that filled your heart with happiness
Now there is the pain of it all
Visiting the past will not bring it back
However it gives the peace in your heart
To accept that you loved and lost
The memories will always remain
The good and the bad ones
To remind you of the love you once shared
It is an empty hole, it's the hole in your heart
You both know it's a broken past, there is no turning back
It cannot be fixed in the present or in the future
The memories will always remain
To give you the strength to continue into the future
Knowing that you loved once, and for a short moment in life you were whole.

Monica Batista

MY SHELTERING WING

Still inside your shell, I loved before I knew you,
As you moved and grew, I imagined who you'd be.
Your feather touch, disguised, what fragile strength can do;
Those eyes and smiles, released, caged feelings within me.

And then afterwards, throughout all those nesting years,
I held your dreams and in long shadows bathed your fears.
Sometimes, I protected you, from becoming prey, Or shared sustaining warmth, through each inclement day.
In one season, I gathered every precious tear,
As life's hard lesson for your fledgling heart, drew near.
Soon, silence was the only answer, I could give,
Because this life from me, belonged to you, to live.

Now flown from this nest, but not my imprinted heart,
Hearing song, I listen, for your distinctive call.
Freedom to explore, some other shore, lets us part;
Still, my sheltering wing is here, if you should fall.

Ingrid Rankin

THE OTHER ME

Within me there's a silent scream,
that others cannot see,
trapped within my deeper self,
I call it the other me.

He hides behind a smile sometimes,
to disguise his inner pain,
a mask of which he has many,
mentally ill . . . but not insane.

His rooms are dark and sigh . . .
a meloncholy upon a wing,
he listens to his music . . .
but never lets anyone in.

His depression has always been,
even before he realised what it was,
it doesn't show like a broken leg,
its inside so deep because.

He doesn't want to feel like this . . .
he often wishes he could die.
head in hands dispairing . . .
why me, oh why, oh why.

The more he fights . . . gloom it falls,
into each restless night,
each moment burns into an hour,
as he tries with all his might.

To reach a dawn few people know,
it lies between two distant places,
one is made of calm and warmth,
the other is cold and hopeless.

Norman Dickson

OLYMPIC BRONZE

When the sculptor Myron asked for me to pose,
I still was breathless from the discus throws.
I tried but found it difficult to hold.
The oil dripped and I slithered on the plinth,
my muscles cramping from the twisted stance.
He steadied me with mottled toad brown hands,
insistent clay caked fingers forcing limbs
to form the angles of the golden mean.
Cast from the cooling mold, I am reborn,
no longer human, almost demi-god.
The light plays on the bronze sheen to define
the tension in my tightened throwing arm
and power in the tapered bulging calf,
a perfect movement frozen for all time.
An idealisation of the human form,
embodiment of all that Plato dreamed,
the line of beauty brought to life through sport
that here below Olympus we all seek
as we compete in honour of the gods.
But bronze statues rust, marble turns to dust,
a crumbling legacy of Hellene art
and our immortal deities will die,
remembered only through a poet's words.
Laurels fade, my name will not survive.
What will survive these remnants of the past
is an ideal to which men may aspire,
a greater gift than any painted vase
or figured fragments from a temple frieze.
For this Olympian vision will endure,
a Golden Age that men may sometimes sense
through focused lenses in an artist's eye
or siren soundings in a poet's voice.

Don Nixon

I CRAWL TO THE BEAT OF THE KITCHEN SINK

The ghost will protect me,
The demon will rip you to shreds.
I am no longer dreaming,
You are no longer screaming.
The hand of the walrus touches me lightly,
The heart of the walrus is inside you.
The entity of the not quite living,
The fusion of thirty-seven souls.
Dance with my corpse.
Dance.
Dance with your corpse.
Dance
Every fracture in my body can be felt.
You are not dead.
The spirit has been eaten.
I have risen. (You have risen)
A blue cloth lay in the snow.
Melting faces on the pavement.
Unknown stickiness.
I am watching. (You are watching)
A red cloth lay in the snow.
They come in pairs.
She hunts with one.
The teeth never smile.
I am fearful (you are fearful)
HFB is the mark on her body.
Renewed is my faith.
Renewed is your faith.
Failure.
I crawl to the beat of the kitchen sink.
Blood in my eyes.
Tears in your eyes.
The uncontrollable mind is coming to haunt *us.*

Nicholas Hintze

SILENCE

it might be stillness
I think it would be a beautiful thing
to be still

The silence
was deeper than the ocean
more secure than the earth

Stillness held me
quietly within the darkness
laid me within the being of my soul

The silence
was profound, stars snapped
in the black endless night

Stillness called to me
sky above quiet
held in suspension by the day

The silence
was stillness quietened
into a greenness of the earth

Teresa Webster

OF BEDS

As the Oyster yields a pearl
man invents.
Neither realises their fecundity
is rooted in irritation:
of one - the body
of the other - the mind.
Man kills the oyster
for its pearl.
And kills his own World
for that *eureka* moment of invention.

Barrie Singleton

THE NEW CORRECT

Let's come together and feel love not pain,

Our ever endearing lives bring us so much mental strain.

Whether it's social, economical or the climate change . . .

Remember as one we are free so to connect is the new correct!

It doesn't matter about your skin colour, to be as one with your global brother . . .

Sisters hold your head up tall, there's no mankind without a mother.

Let's put our differences aside and see our bond in full affect.

Remember as one we are free so to connect is the new correct.

It don't matter what technology puts inside our sight full minds,

You will find that back to basics is the way forward for us to shine.

And the wise one may bring you wisdom, turn life's zigzags into a line.

So remember as one we are free so to connect is the new correct!

Wesley

SUBLIMINAL

The message was clear
Although my heart was beating as if from fear
My joy produced a tear
All this because you were near

My chest did a dance
As if my heart were attempting an Irish prance
My eyes all a dazed as though I were in a trance
All this just from a glance

The palpitations
Born from intense beautiful situations
My heart nor head fathoming any complications
I was ready for you and I would not accept any limitations

It's all happened in such a short space of time
Your heart I shall conquer, like Mount Everest I did climb
For you are as fine as an uncut dime
Subliminally it's because my heart has fallen, you are sublime.

Dee Makanda

A JOY FOREVER

Let the beacon shine
Through desolation's chilling void
Under the howling tempest of treachery

That beacon is your soul
Forever nourished
Graced channel for all love and beauty
Flowing through the centuries

I see through dark zones of future dread;
Through cyclic time to your prime radiance

Should we once have had
A strangers' tryst
To gel the crystals of our memories?

The crystal is there, centering the beacon's flame
The crystal is, encases
Your beauty's everlasting light
Breathed, ever aired
Core of my memory

Dreams' flashes made you Aphrodite
Glistening with the luminous waters

On with your girdle – to charge your loins
With incandescence;
As you rippled, shimmered through it
Your magnetism rose
To overwhelming voltage

So potent fertiliser of my fires

As I undo your girdle, I am charged
Our energies in tandem, then collide –
A short-circuit of perfection
The sparks ignite succeeding energy
Life's flow into the purified millennia

Distilled eternity
Forever sensual in the spirit

David Russell

SWEET FAMILY MEMORIES

You're my Mother and my best friend
You taught me how to dream and hope
No matter what life throws at me
I know that I can cope

You gave me the very best start in life
Family always played a big part
The fun we had, the things we did
Are memories I treasure safely in my heart

Gran, Papa, Dad, Judy, you and I
Packed up in the car for a drive
Not knowing where we'd end up
In the rain or with midges eating us alive

We went for walks along the shore
The picnics in the rain
And I'd give all my tomorrows
To have just one of those days again.

Paula Marion R Jackson

SPRINGTIME SONNET

And now they're withering to faded beauty,
each sunrise setting, crumpled to decay.
No coward spirits, crushed, they did their duty
as orbs of hopefulness sent on their way

to seed the earth with golden daffodils,
because their gleaming sunbeams pleasured, pleased.
Yet these were born to die on window sills.
No nectar buzzes bumbled in, nor breezed

to barrenness, as beauty – gone – despairs.
They live without their children: empty wombs,
remaining homed, their earthliness compares
with drying corms. Too premature, their tombs

fattening with dreams and moisture. Bled
to words that shake the stars until they're dead.

Wendy Webb

GULF WAR

Another world where time stands still,
A lunar scene, barren and bleak.
From daytime heat to night-time chill,
All far too tired to want to speak.
Full of injections, feeling sore,
Sprayed all around while in their tent.
Sand in their socks and pants (and more!)
Morning is near, the night is spent.
Camels, snakes and scorpions too,
Arabian desert harsh and rough.
Sun in a sky of endless blue,
Nature intends to make it tough!
Requests for things we use each day,
Tooth and paint brush, towel and bowl.
Condoms (for rifles!) and games to play,
Needle and wool to darn a hole.
No map or compass by which to steer,
Out on 'detail' and getting lost.
Syrian camps not giving much cheer
When wandering in like sand blown ghost.
Red cross arm bands, where were they?
Like map and compass, left behind,
Making it hard for men to obey
The rules of war, to follow blind.
Jubayl and Ryadh 'up the road',
Kuwait the goal for which they aim.
Tanks and trucks with their heavy load,
No looking back from whence they came.
The midday black from burning oil,
The eerie glowing pillars of fire,
Purposely lit and meant to spoil
By mad Hussein, his warped desire
To win the war. He should have known
He could not beat the British force
Against such might, he stood alone,
They'd grind him down with no remorse.
Launching missiles, chemical alarm,
So much noise with no chance to sleep.
Constant attack to do most harm,
Friend and foe having cause to weep.
Miles from Iraq on Christmas day,
Plenty of sand but not a drink.
Keep sense of humour come what may,
Write a letter while time to think.

Basra road and on to Kuwait,
Warehouse complex camp 'til they leave.
Pleased to find they were not too late,
Did what they came for, time to relieve.
Use of ambulance helping them out,
Not just the wounded, but sick as well.
Duties finished, then turn about,
Head for home away from the hell.
Young men and old, tired from the war,
The sand, the heat, all it entailed.
Time to relax, forget what they saw,
But proud to know they never failed.

Ann Odger

THE NIGHT IS COLD THE NIGHT IS LONG

The night is cold the night is long
You walk alone amongst the throng
A passing train's flickering windows
Becomes a hypnotic kaleidoscope
Clitter-clatter, clitter-clatter
Doesn't matter, doesn't matter
Echoes around and round your mind
Its wheels of metal screech and grind
Nearby buskers ply their trade
Faster faster round and round
Dancing dancing to the crowd
The night is cold the night is long
But still you manage to sing a song
Your footsteps echo all around
You feel the vibrations on the ground
The piercing sound of a howling cat
Is joined by the trains hooting horn
Then silence falls all around
Till you cannot hear a single sound
Except the beating of your heart
Thumping thumping in your chest
Echoing echoing in your head
The night is cold the night is long

D M Walford

FALLEN IN 1918

Pulling and heaving the sandbags
Making it tight
To block the dam and help the fight
Tolling for hours within the sound
Of the guns
Working for King and country
No time to run

Watching and waiting for the
The enemy to draw near
Lookouts on the alert nothing
To fear
Labouring hard sweat on
Our brows
Hearing the Captain bellow
Orders aloud

Standing proud on the baulks
With the timber bending
Tired hands and feet all
together defending
Stacking the bags to stem
The water flow
Six to eight hundred sandbags
Pulled through the mud and
Ready to go

Suddenly, panic, the piers
start to crumble
feet losing stability taking a tumble
Sandbags and sappers into the
river below
Shouts from the Captain
sod the sandbags, men, danger
go go go!

Every attempt was made
To recover
The sappers who had fallen
In May 1918
Others stood helpless
And watched from the whaling
Hoping and praying
That the last would be seen

After dredging the water
Late into the night
One single sapper remained
missing out of sight
The outcome of war had claimed
another brave man
Not missing in action
But drowned in a foreign land

Anne Hulbert

PUPPET OF THE CAULDRON

If Satan was to pick from the bubbling cauldron,
A puppet for his mischievous play
Called from home to dance before the Devil's hand
And turn the purest mixture of the kind
From beautiful blue and glowering green
To tainted trouble and blackened filth.

A rapid spit from the cauldron like a stutter from a machine gun
Below the puppet swings from a sudden explosion
of sound, a response to the Devil's work and
continued rumbling from the pit.
Waxed, wailing souls filtered from the cauldron
and escaped from the Hell, dying as martyrs.
Six million spirits continued to follow them
to a higher tier of the afterlife.
Satan's eyes gleamed with greed.

The puppet's sinful smile began to
change corners to a grave grimace.
The fire of a single pistol shot rang
off the pot. The Devil howled in rage.
Muffled cheers sounded out of the broil.
The puppet's life had gone and
its small moustache and cropped hair wilted
While the swastika faded on its jacket.
The foul broth turned to pure again.
The Holocaust had ended.

Sam Riley

TROUBLE BREATHING

I was a good swimmer,
But I had trouble
breathing,
My body was strong,
and
my legs were powerful,
but
I panted and
coughed
all the air out,
and struggled
to grasp oxygen.
I could go
hard,
for a couple of
lengths,
but then I'd
sink.

'He's a good singer,
But he has trouble
breathing,
He can hold a note,
and
there's gusto in his voice,
but
it doesn't last long and
he goes a little flat,
or completely
out of tune.'

I wanted to be a great
boxer,
But I had trouble
breathing,
I could jab, uppercut
and
swing, I was fast as
hell too,
but
I didn't have the stamina and
once the wind was
knocked out,
there was only
shit, and

after the shit was
knocked out,
I'd hit the
deck.

But I didn't get to
swimming much, and
I hated to sing, and
the only fights I ever
had were in the streets, and
they didn't pay, just cost.
So if you're waiting for
a semi-aquatic siren
who fights like the best of
them,
Don't hold your breath.

Ian Critchley

STEREOTYPICAL

The world is a stereotypical place
Judgments on every action of the human race
A scratch on the head
Means they have nits on their bed
The use of slang
Means there stupid instead
Every accent and action screams out for analysis

But what if I took your smile.
Without assuming you had gone to bed with another
Saw your watery eye.
And didn't assume that you were sad
But, how can it work   this   breaking of human instinct.
And even if we didn't say it.
We would still be thinking it instead.
Until we go crazy, with it going round and round in our head.

Susannah Rooke

HOOKED IN HER OWN ARMS

She waited in line at the paying desk,
for self-service help from the dead,

on legs the shape of question marks,

and please take your items now, ma'am,

in the little corner shop round back of her head,
where the unborn thoughts were aborted,

culled for clothing

behind blacked-out windows
the colour of white,

and how she wished the sun would set

so finally set!

on the sign post she waits by
marked exit,

this way and that

and bleed its orange glow on dank streets
where rain fills gaps between
the stolen church flagstones,

the cyanide lacing the drink she cradles,

it is her own little London,

housed inside
the little corner shop round back of her head,

where hollow eggs that hatched were sold,
processed, but of course,

and battery-powered puppets that walked,
tired of string tight husband and wife games,

all bartered for with hand gestures,
like sign language to the blind,

and her gown was only touched
caressed, I think it was,

with dirt the shade of greenery,
that entered the frayed lace without moving,
penetrating deep,
and teasing off material with filth from forgotten bed sheets,

she was just another rose without a root,

until she was dressed alone in her nakedness,

or a tutu that waltzes her along
an abandoned high street of tumbleweeds
all singing her name,

and still stumbling to meet the opening,
the opening wide –

to know that everything must go!

the sign says so itself!
she sees it written so in caesura,

– into new homes that are always empty,

and claustrophobic in a crowd of her,
as she plays with teardrops still glistening on her false plastic lashes –

just a pound sign and a make-believe kiss,

now mirror, mirror, on my own wall, whose the weakest of them all –

like tainting history out of class,

with weak rubber bands
wrapped around bubbles in an endless tub she floats in,

on that strange day the world arranged a photograph
that she was allowed to keep –

the price had seemed so very fair,
just another length of her waterless pool –

and she wore knee-high boots right up to the toes,
a see-through top that saw nothing,

her hands worked, labourers that wolf-whistled,
little mating sounds to the palms,

and to herself that had been there oh so long,
that time itself had walked away still counting its change;
the tips of each dying strand of hair,

a little bleached noose with dusted ties
here, there, everywhere,

had been dipped in the cold puddles of old age
that wait in prison cells built of lost walking sticks,

like a mannequin turned away in a shop window.

She is caught with bloodied bait in her fishnet tights,
wondering

forever wondering

why so many roads weren't marked on the map,
why so many hiding places were unearthed,

no longer able to hide in her own little deaths.

And here at the self-service help desk,

do you still stock these?
a pair of handcuffs rusted in her palm,

from seven years waiting,

she is just a footnote,
an error in the margin,

who says again

and again

'I'd be better off trading with myself.'

Christopher Glover

UNINHABITED

Alone.
Standing silently
amongst antiquated echoes,
cool, still air, carries insubstantial fancies,
looming shadows of past presences.

Light shimmers like a gossamer thread
dancing genteelly between alabaster pillars,
tangibly trembling,
ghosting then fading.

Tantalisingly inaudible rustles prick my senses
creating tenuous, diaphonous links in my mind,
I turn.
Holding my breath.
To meet hidden histories.

Goosebumps rise.
A faint flicker of fragile tangibility weaves a welcome of delight
before settling to soundless tranquillity.

P Baker

DON'T TAKE YOUR LOVE FROM ME

(With acknowledgement to Henry Nemo, who wrote the song 'Don't Take Your Love From Me')

Take away my furniture from me,
my costly china and my silverware,
my carpets and also my curtains,
all the gifts I've ever received,
my stores of books and records,
don't take your love from me

Take away all my favourite dishes,
the drinks that quench my thirst,
the foods that nourish my body,
sweets, ice cream, honey and cake,
the pleasures of taste and smell,
don't take your love from me

Take away all my credit cards,
the money in my bank account,
all my gold and valuable jewels,
the expensive clothes that I wear,
my stocks and shares and bonds,
don't take your love from me

Take the paintings from my walls,
all my sculptures from their plinths,
the music that I enjoy hearing,
poetry that always lifts my spirits,
the films I see on screens,
don't take your love from me

Take away the moon and stars,
the glow and warmth of sunshine,
the clouds and also the rain,
the trees and grass and bushes,
the bright colours of the flowers,
don't take your love from me

Take away my hopes and dreams,
all the memories I hold dear,
my youth, my health and strength,
my certainty about what I believe,
my empathy with all living creatures,
don't take your love from me

Neville Davis

NEVER ENDING

Trees a-blowing
On the water's edge
Whispering willows
And the overgrown hedge.
Listen to the winds
Calling to the leaves
Fluttering around
And falling off the trees.

Petals opening up
Trying to touch the sun
The flowing of the sea
Where all life first began.
The sun and the moon
Side by side
Like a son, and a daughter,
Since time and evolution began
Mothering the earth
Bringing us
Its beauty of nature.

The sky in all its glory
Has been put there
For a reason,
Opening up when it cries
So the flowers all around us
Keep on growing and never die.
The sun keeps on shining
The moon leaves shadows
On the still waters,
Buds keep on budding
Mother Nature
Just astound us.

Have you ever stopped to listen?
Just how silence
Is almost heard,
You can hear the silence
On one note,
Beside the humming of the birds.

Who knows what will happen
In the here now, or the future,
But one thing
You can be sure of,
There will always be
'Mother Nature!'

Mary Woolvin

WATERFALL

Trickling stream, cascading
down stone slab steps,
from moorland foliage
into that sudden drop.

Into the pool below
half-filled with debris
of broken stone washings,
splashing with echoing sound.

Then over more rocky steps,
enlarged to streaming overflow
as the depth responds
to more rain above.

Wider, ever widening,
the brook becomes a stream, then
a rock-strewn river torrent
bursting into the lands below.

Thus, the little waterfall –
and others like it –
in deluged tributary flows
become the mother of a flood.

Rising up across field and village;
homeless human neighbours
now confer, how at last
to build again, flood waters to deter.

Life must go on, in its own way
like the essential water flows
that also bring life
to all Earth's creatures.

Jo Allen

FESTIVAL OF DEBT

There's a festival today in Erdington,
Pay-day loans have arrived,
Handed out with free balloons,
Into the hands of the deprived.

Balloons blowing on the high street,
And ready to be handed out,
To children in passing buggies,
And toddlers toddling about.

But parents you are the target, As you reach for a free balloon,
Making debt family-friendly,
Both quick and opportune.

Hip, hip hooray, we're happy
We're hanging out the flags,
We're marching along the high street,
Swinging our carrier bags.

We march to a debtor's tune.
We sing a debtor's song,
We wave our bright balloons,
As we merrily march along.

Making it family fun,
High on helium laughs
Welcome to the debt explosion,
Shown on spiralling graphs.

Of economic trends,
And post-boom busts,
Of lack of self-control,
Turning our wants into our musts.

The Big Bang detonation,
As balloons burst in the street,
The sense of trepidation,
That rocks the balance sheet.

Hip, hip hooray, we're happy
We're hanging out the flags,
We're marching along the high street,
Swinging our carrier bags.

We march to a debtor's tune.
We sing a debtor's song,
We wave our bright balloons,
As we merrily march along.

Our hopes have been inflated,
Our aspirations way too high,
We should learn about self-control,
And when to be satisfied.

When the helium happiness is spread about,
And laughter lifts the mood,
The giggles that the children show,
Take our mind off being shrewd

We're celebrating a carnival,
With ribbon and bunting too,
Everything is so colourful
In the red with the payday blues.

Hip hip hooray, we're happy
We're hanging out the flags,
We're marching along the high street,
Swinging our carrier bags.

We march to a debtor's tune.
We sing a debtor's song,
We wave our bright balloons,
As we merrily march along.

But somehow the gaiety jars,
It strikes a grating note,
It's the sugar on the pill,
That sticks inside your throat.

You don't want to seem negative,
You don't want to spoil the mood,
You may feel you should be grateful,
When you're really feeling screwed.

But surely one day soon,
We know the balloon will burst
At festival time in Erdington,
You look for salvation and find you're cursed.

Chris Lee

I SAW A UFO THIS MORNING

I saw a UFO this morning
The government said it was global warming
Just pollution in the sky, a trick of the eye
The newsreader said so shifty and sly
I saw a UFO this morning
They beamed me up aboard
Attached me to a strange machine
As I dangled from a cord
I saw a UFO this morning
I looked at the Earth from above
A creature penetrated my mind
And we started making love
I saw a UFO this morning
And we travelled round the globe
They took samples of my blood and skin
And used a ten foot anal probe
I saw a UFO this morning
Now I'm walking like John Wayne
They asked me why we destroy our planet
Why humans are insane
I saw a UFO this morning
And we flew into the sun
Past meteors and star systems
We played I spy just for fun
I saw a UFO this morning
Now I have lost track of time
The creatures planned to help the Earth
But now they've changed their minds
Because of the human way, selfless decay
Corporate greed, planting the seed
Illegal wars, fascist laws, hate not love
Humanity deserves everything it's got
So they've left us alone on this Earth to rot
I saw a UFO this morning
The government said it was global warming
Just pollution in the sky, a trick of the eye
The newsreader said so shifty and sly

Tom Quinton

WE MUST

To be brave, we must have fear,
To listen, we must hear,
To have faith, we must believe,
To laugh, we must breathe,
To dream, we must imagine,
To cry, we must have emotion,
To hurt, we must feel,
To stay alive, we must heal,
To break apart, we must fall,
To be strong, we must stand tall,
To love, we must have passion,
To achieve, we must have ambition,
To lose, we must fail,
To win, we must prevail,
To pray, we must hope,
To survive, we must cope,
To explain, we must understand,
To help, we must lend a hand,
To learn, we must make mistakes,
To live, we must do what it takes,
To fight, we must be bold,
To be cruel, we must be cold,
To change, we must see inside,
To move forward, we must decide,
To take action, we must make a choice,
To speak up, we must have a voice.

Charlotte Beaumont-McAllen

FISHERMAN

A statue, under stone clouds
in the shovelled, sleet-steel sky
by the concrete pool
of frozen, still-stuck fish,
sits the fisherman.

And all those greys rest
in every line in his concentrated face,
to narrow-away his downward chin
and the crag-lines mapping
the pale of his fine, fixed eyes.

Unflinching, unmoving; he won't be moved.
And there is security in his wrist,
tied to the stiff sinew of his forearm
which, weighted, hangs at the shoulder,
where every socket is ground, immobile.

The plane-waters are solemn, inaction
and the fisherman hardly lets his heart beat.

And silence builds behind him,
through him it surges, like quiet winds,
fearing to strip the semblance
of calm and called-for poise
matched only in the trunks of buried, rooted trees.

But, explosion! And the line's a whirr!
His eyes erupt in flames
which charge the fire in that fine forelock,
as forearms work as new, emblazoned
by the automatic memory of pulling.

Then, the spinning, buzzing reel disturbs
and competes for air-space,
drowning out poor-voiced, brethren bees
and piercing ears to the point of bleeding,
ruining the silence, known only moments before.

Watch the kiln-eyes burning in the fisherman's skull,
intensely focussed on the diamond line,
where it invades the water's skin
like an unwanted maggot, burrowing
and rooting in the perfect ear to a perfect mind.

That stare starts the water foaming.
There's magic, found deep, in the patience.
Bubbling, spurting, a mouth-curse spittle,
the surface belches and throws-up
a fish, of weight, and worth unknown,

Enough to force a smile from the eyes,
to the mouth, of the tireless fisherman.

Steven Jackson

GHOST DOGS

The wolves hunt me down to the song of the Arctic.
They howl under a moonlit sky,
for my soul, thin and icy.

They slide slowly, silent grey shimmers.
I run from them, through icy lands and lakes,
my bones burned to stone.

Survival of the fittest is the game,
loss of strength, loss of sight,
ghost dogs in night shadows.

Another day. Ravens follow me overhead,
drops of blood fall –
like berries.

I open my eyes, waters still there is no sound.
I rest with my conscience. Time to feast,
time to fight this beast.

The Pole Star shivers through winds,
guides me towards clearer plains.
I prowl with my cubs through the mist.
We roam together in a fanged pack.

Nicola Holden

YOU ARE

My beloved husband
I remember our most beautiful day
Our wedding
It was the best day of my life
Marrying my best friend and my soulmate
We didn't let the rain spoil our day
Until God had decided to take you
To a much beautiful and better place
Called Sweet Heaven
Now that you have gone
Leaving me all alone
With a broken heart
And tears are rolling down my face
Wishing that I had gone too
But you are now my most beautiful Guardian Angel
With your most beautiful and gorgeous halo
And your beautiful Angel wings
Wrapped around me giving me
All the love and protection
Feeling your Angel kisses on my lips
You will always be with me
Until God calls my name
That's when I know you've come to take me
Home again for me to wrap my loving arms
Around you
Giving you all my love and happiness
That you have missed while you have been gone
I will be dancing with all the Angels
And all my loved ones
To be with you once again
You are the sun that shines down
Into my loving heart and soul
You are the most beautiful shining star
That shines down onto me
And you are the rain that falls down
From my eyes onto my face
but we will always be married
and that true love never dies
we will be together again one day

Jennie Webster

THE KISS TO SAY THE WORDS, YOUR LIPS CANNOT

As the wooden door closed
returning to its place of rest
with little more than a soft thud,
I kissed her,
using the kiss instead of words
trying to tell her I loved her,
and I think she understood,
our hands moving over each other,
mine down by her waist
and hers on my chest,
still engaged in the kiss,
I moved my hand
into the back pocket of her jeans
and gave a gentle squeeze,
she responded
by pulling me closer,
so close I could feel
her heart beat in my chest,
leading her down to the bed
lips still locked together,
still spelling out
the verses in my heart's love song,
breaking only to pull my top
over my head.
Our naked bodies
now pressed together,
sharing warmth
and love,
two people making love
because of love,
all the time still locked
in a kiss,
and when our bodies
had been to that state of ecstasy,
slowly our lips parted,
and we laid there
side by side,
and she leant over and kissed my lips,
a kissed that answered mine,
a kiss that said, I love you too.

Andrew Evans

LOVE

Love is worth saving I think you should know
But if we never fall in Love then how can we grow
How can an hour feel like a day?
When the person you Love is so far away
When you hope that that person feels the same too
That that person is sitting there thinking the same about you
That it'll all be alright you'll see in the end
That Love is worth sharing and to us it will send
A message of hope that will see our way through
But after all's said and done, we know what to do
We take it and hold it and make it grow strong
And keep it together so it never goes wrong
We think of the days when we laugh and hold hands
And think of the Love that is cleansing our Lands
Think of the times when you're bursting with Joy
You feel like a child with their first Christmas toy
You think of the time that's coming our way
And hoping that Love is coming to stay
But we've been there n done that and let's not pretend
That Love is our saviour, our guidance, our friend
Love can be rotten and hurtful and cruel
So when it raises its head, you know it's a duel
But you have to sit back and let it fit like a glove
Open the door and welcome in
Love

please

Mole

BLACK WIDOW

Your lips are poison to my senses
Making me jump over fire engulfed fences
Your touch kills me with every imprint
Tasting you is acid yet I still want to drink
I fear you have stolen my unforgiving mind
Squeezing it between your fingers is somewhat divine
Suffocate me with your womanly powers
A weeping willow grows strong amongst your stormy showers
Feeling my heart strangulated by your presence
Your moonlit body glimmers an eerie florescence
Shortness of breath weakens my guard
Powerless by your beauty and my morals are tarred
A black widow that you are,
Leaving this moment a mental scar.

Adele Simone Pierce

THE TRANSPLANT

To hospital I went – I had an accident
I chopped off my penis with a knife
If I was feeling bad for the accident I'd had
I wasn't half as disappointed as my wife

With the wonders of modern microsurgery
Doctors have performed a transplant
They couldn't find anything more suitable
So they grafted on the trunk of an elephant

Now I don't want to sound ungrateful
Don't get me wrong I won't complain
But my life is not enhanced by a trunk in my pants
Sometimes I must confess it is a pain

For example, having soup inside a Café
A stick of crusty bread just makes me glum
Cos then to my surprise it emerges from my flies
Steals a roll and shoves it up my bum

Bob Gessey

PSILOCYBIN AWAKENING TO ENTER A NEW WORLD

Two by two they enter leaving a taste so foul
Though they satisfy that eternal hunger
The two of us united to go on a journey to unify our souls
Married in a strange world we sort another
To redefine our essence as lovers
Physic abilities remained distance
Enhancement would allow us to embrace ourselves
Feeling nausea we touch our hearts
Becoming unwell though more well than ever
That sensation of first witnessing soap lather
The foam and the way it seems heavenly as it disables
Resembles the now translucent walls of the room
We stretch to touch
Though touch seems unnecessary in this new reality
Colours dance before our eyes
Golden rays, crimson reds
Unite to become an orange haze
We see our eyes look back at us
Have we left our bodies and moved to another world?
We inhale to become light
Eyelashes flutter like a bird in flight
Exhaling we hold each other's hands and soar
Joined by a majestic dove
We glide in the air
The world is afar
Unknown be this planet
Enveloped in a place with no land
We try to focus, though stay perplexed
This glory where we communicate in mind
Move like data through cables
We appreciate without understanding
Simply being
Primordial world that has taken no shape
It remains spontaneous in movement
Leading us to be together and fly
The dove perches on a cloud
Wingspan open
We enter to be embraced

A trickle dances down our spine
Expanded mind
Entwined love
This mystery
Brings you next to me
How can we return to that world?
Now that we are awaken
A vision can be our reality

Louis Cecile

LAST TIME I WERE AT THIS PLACE

It seems inconvenient that I should revert,
Back to the past after so much progress to convert,
My mind to the state it was once in,
Way before it had been drenched by this sin.

The day after this I am going back to a place,
Which has an intrinsic association with his face,
And I fear for my mind now so sound,
After weeks, months where no sanity could be found.

All I can recall is walking along the beach,
With him in mind and all he did teach,
Declaring my unwritten commitment upon sands
Which we would later seal by merely holding hands.

But all this was so long ago,
Who once was a lover is now a foe,
And though I may tolerate fond memories of a kiss,
I will refuse to say it is he I miss.

This time when I watch the landscape bled by the sun,
I will block from my mind what is now done,
This time when I return to this place,
It is only my own insecurity I will face.

Victoria Maguire

GUIDANCE

The wind rallies the sand
calling,
it surges forward
across my cheeks and eyes.
Dunes moved with ease
through the desolation,
piled in the shadow of man's genius.
Fossilised stones are shaped, torn
by the chill of these winter nights.

The jackal salivates at my feet,
his grin, his cackle,
bounces back from the horizon
lingers in the rising sun.
His filthy fur raised
like folded hands to heaven.
His tongue is warm
but his eyes-
your face on his drooling carcass.

Great God of spirits with open jaws,
I charge you:
Speak of man's invention.
Let me build you temples
to rival the afterlife.

You howl
an echo across the sand.

Dust turns into ruby rivers,
pooling at the jackal's paws.
The blood of children, women's salt
and man's back laid these foundations.
Stone by stone
carved on Pharaoh's whim,
Did you lay him with the slaves?
Will you lay me with him?

Rebecca Lodder

IMAGE IS ALWAYS IMPORTANT.

You were my brand new camera of a high pixel and a close up lens.
With shiny features which would encourage my delicate touch to treat you with such a respect, that everyone would know I was proud.
You were my gift. Not to *use*, but to *have* and hold and care after.
Your smile, flash and relapse would trap me in a grasp, a grasp so tight that only you could control who sees us, and adores.
There was no developing stage for you. You were already finished.
So untainted by your image, for you only captured the creatures you desired and cast away those who had disgusted you.
However I was a little different. You bought be at the rejected section of Boots where the outdated lingered and loitered.
I was your disposable throw away. I had paper to protect me, and my inners were cheap and plastic which easily melted under your radiant sun.
I too had the ability to flash and capture, but I always had an element of mystery in the process of doing this.
I had no control of my outcome. I tried to develop and reveal the goodness inside.
But more often than not, the gifts I revealed were cast aside once you had cast your sharp eye over them.
We were both the same you and I, of the same type.
The only difference being that you were never temporary. But I think I was to you.

Caleb Assirati

THE PAIN OF MY LONELINESS

Days became weeks,
Weeks became months and
Months Became years!
Come and see what state I am in without you
I roam around like a crazy girl,
I live but I don't die,
I take the pain of my loneliness
Night and day!
Come, come, come,
I will count the days till you come!

Arosa Ahmed

THE LOVE LIE

Other poems and quotes
Leave the misleading view behind
That love is a one way boat
The non-ending ocean ride
But that isn't true
Love lied to you

Terminating the brain
Finding another half of you,
But that's its game
Love isn't a part of you

Love isn't through
Its just coming back for you
Love isn't invincible
Love is just a criminal

Love isn't lovely
Love is a lie
Love isn't everything
Love is a disguise

Love is 'the world'
Love is in every view
But that isn't true
Love is just a world stronger than you

Mariah Lee-Davis

MURMURATION

There's a murmuring in the sky,
a dark cloud whooshing, sighing,
above a skyline of trees, they come,
turning this way and that.

Sounds of many wings, coming closer, ever closer,
shape shifting above a sloping hill,
one mind, one body,
telepathic thought in flight.

Once again the sky darkens,
they fall as one entity, to roost overnight.

A star twinkles in a naked sky.

Josephine Smith

FLASHBACKS

It's been six long years since I did my last tour, I didn't know how much would endure I left the forces and Afhan and Iraq, never again would I want to go back
Those war-torn countries I am far away, but yet in my head those countries do stay
Now I'm a civilian I've went from job to job, why can't I hold a single one, what is it I've lost?
I could cross the street and the shouting I hear, I can look around and no one is near
I can go to the park in the light or dark, combat I see a my mind flashes back
Crowded streets people pushing past, everything slows down sometimes it goes fast
In numerous stores I've stacked countless shelves, flashes come of the war-torn hell
I see families of friends who didn't make it back, once endless conversations which now we lack
In gridlocked roads car horns sound, is the enemy near? I start to look around
I close my eyes at night the dead I see, every single night they come to me
I'm at a loss of what I can do, I've tried all sorts of help and there's nothing new
I was at home and now I'm lost, leaving the forces is an unimaginable cost
Being a civilian is a new way of life, I think to myself it's an unnecessary strife
I have a gun under lock and key, but too many times I've thought of using it on me
There is no family like brothers in arms, we could face death together and still carry on with charm
Being a civilian I feel so alone, I have a house but it's not my military home
Why do I find it hard to adjust, me leaving the forces was it really a must?
Every day I struggle through, but as I hear troops flying to combat but I want to go
I have cleaned my weapon a Beretta nine mil, I find it relaxing and it helps me to chill
With hollow point round the magazine is filled, it's about this point where I can no longer chill
Into the handle the magazine slides, the tears at this point I find hard to hide
I cock the weapon and chamber a round, the firing of my weapon should be my last sound
I place the muzzle under my chin, I can feel in the weapon that my skin is so thin
On the trigger my finger moves, if I squeeze it now what will it prove?
My hand shakes as my finger goes tight, what am I doing it is wrong or right?
I think of graves which I have come to know, they died as honourable men that we all know
If I take my own life what does that make me? Would I be a coward? Is that what people would see?
I take out the magazine eject the chambered round, this isn't the way I want to be found
The images of comrades both wounded and dead, will forever more stay burned in my head
What of the person who will discover me, it's not an image I want them to see
I'll live with the shouting the guns and the bomb, I'll see my dead friends although it is wrong
I'll remember the horrors which I see day and night, and for now it seems I'll live another night.

Gordon Bruce

BACKWARDS

Feel curious,
giddy,
waiting for
the moment -
Trapped in
bottled glass,
as if
I'm trying
to hold it.

The blood in me,
shaking,
sinking,
breaks
Against the skin
Of your fingertips,
trace over
my face.

Breathing
beside you,
seeing
shapes
in the dark,
I can't do
this now
'I can't
feel my heart.'

Falling in love
backwards
with you
closer,
harder
than I ever
meant to

Kirsty Grant

GRANDMA'S MEMORY BOX

I sit here looking in to a memory box
Smiling at the good times
I sit and then think
What's that number I rang so many times?
It plays on my mind, but why?
It's not like you will answer

But then it hits me
And here comes that awful pain
That pain everyone says will soon fade
But then, if it fades
Does this mean my only memory of you
Will be sat here looking in this memory box?

Now the tears start to slowly fall
As I remember what I have lost
So I close my eyes and go back in time
I put on your cardigan and smell your smell
But sadly it's fading

I think back to the world I lived in
With you so perfect it was like it was not real
Then I remember that awful day
That day for everyone else is about love and joy
But for me it's a constant reminder of the love and joy I lost
On Valentine's day
And how I never got to say my last proper goodbye

So I think back to the pain I felt that day
When I got that call to tell me I lost you
I don't know why but I can't get it out of my mind
Why did I not say goodbye?
I took it for granted that you will always be there
But if I had my chance to say goodbye
I would never say it

Now I look to the sky when night falls
And pick out the shiniest star and smile
Hoping and thinking it's you to this day
And forever more I hope one day
I will get my last goodbye
Then start it again
With a smile.

Jade Amanda Headland

COSMIC WIND

It blew so gently
Yet so strong
This Cosmic Wind sang its song.

The message of hope it gave in tune
To save the Earth, Sun and Moon

The people listened and still they became
Bewitched by the magic of the cosmic rain

Enlightened at last they saved this Earth
By conscious thought they saw its worth

So this Cosmic Wind with its power
Changed the days
The seconds
And the hour

A different existence will come to be
So humanity lives peacefully
Wise and free

Pamela Dickson

THE MAN I NOW CALL MINE - REECE LEWIS

I'm falling, and falling fast
you have been in my life so shortly
yet it already feels I have come to my decision
I wish it to be a life time.

It scares me, excites me, confuses me
I am always in control mentally and emotionally
. . . not this time
but it's okay, I understand this now.
I know you don't feel yourself to be in control
you are not like that, you are different
Never to expose or exploit the weakness I now have.

I'm falling . . . but hiding my fall
I cannot show you . . . yet I will.

Nadine Buttigieg

COOL BEANZ

I am lost somewhere on Planet Earth
Where people talk a language strange to me.
I see familiar sights for what they're worth
Trapped inside a time warp with no key.

The supermarket queue goes back a mile,
Shuffling army dressed in faded jeans;
Cashier working swiftly minus smile,
I thank her and she replies 'Cool beanz'.

I struggle with a text from teenage son.
He has an interview 2moz, he wrote.
It's not that I have lost my sense of fun;
It's just that I don't understand his note.

A BTW an OMG
I worked it out eventually.
Dat fin wid u
What thing with me?
U no wot ur lyk
Said he.

I sat there in a bemused state
I think he meant I couldn't read.
He disappeared with his m8.
Now this made me slightly aggrieved.

I took my dog for a brief walk,
Wrapped up warm against the snow;
The postman stopped to have a talk
'Has someone taken your mojo?'

'They might well have,' I forced a grin
And hurried home, despite the ice.
I tried to find the meaning then,
Looked up my Oxford Concise.

There is no 'soz' in Mansfield Park.
Did Shakespeare pen Midsummer Nite . . .?
Byron, Keats, they made their mark
And probably spelt most words right.

Thanx 2 dis tho, coz I'm no fool,
I quickly learnt what it all means,
With one exception to the rule -
Can someone help me with 'cool beanz'?

Helen Somers

MR MELBOURNE

He wakes when I can no longer
hold off sleep.
The Earth's our child wedge.
Though older,
I run like a hamster
to he who mirrors my past mind
in the future.

I remember last night's landscapes.
With the dark go the darkest thoughts,
but the space between
eye and hand is dangerous.

I am inevitably intimate with the unknown
whose work I have inherited
in his still pumping heart,
like a ruinous building.

The colony,
weird theme park of childhood towns,
plays host Germany raised in Australia,
Iran raised in England,
both appreciating a pool's leniency
where one can hold another, weightless,
against a not nuclear sun.
The rest is arguments.

I would never have forgotten
something I could touch.
Affection is carnal,
like bleeding,
like death,
nature loves a cycle.
He pitied me with his next breath.

Setareh Ebrahimi

THE OTHER SIDE

Things will get better,
They always do.
Stand up for what you believe in,
For what you know is true.
Don't be afraid of being heard,
Don't be afraid to fight,
Fight for the people you love,
Fight with all your might.
Don't let the fear of losing keep you down,
Fight back and use your voice.
She was hurting and I had to make it stop,
So I found my courage and made the right choice.
A new found strength I didn't know I had,
Did that really come from me?
I fight for those that I love,
I am finally free.
Don't be afraid of getting hurt,
Because when you come out the other end you'll be that much stronger.
I was so worried and afraid I'd let her down,
Now I know we'll be friends forever and longer.
Throughout life you may be thrown a few curveballs,
But life is just one big roller-coaster ride.
Don't run away from life though,
Or you could end up missing the good parts while you hide.
There are bullies, people and events that will try to pull you down,
This is my life and I'm going to embrace it cause it's mine and I know that inside.
It's okay to feel sad sometimes, but give your heart a break,
Take time to be who you are and just shine.
I know what it's like in that horrible place,
I've been there on the other side.
When you feel so alone like no one is there for you,
Not even the people you love.
In a place so dark you think you're to blame so you punish yourself,
I'm not religious but back then I'd pray every night and look above.
But there is a light at the end of the tunnel,
And the sun will shine again.
And even if it's only for a while,
There is no more pain.
So stand up and be heard,
Stand up and shout as loud as you can.
Don't let fear rule your life,
Be strong and be proud of who you are man!

Natassia Caitlan Cole

THE BITTER SWEET

Now hush be still,
White angel's will,
She cools my fevered brow.
Calm creating,
I lay waiting,
Not now my child, not now

The pains begin,
This life within,
Won't wait another day.
Reassurance,
Such endurance,
As nature has its way.

No baby's cry,
No reason why,
Into this world you came.
Then swept away,
A time to pray,
Am I the one to blame?

Hospital bed,
My aching head,
The overwhelming pain.
Feel like dying,
No child lying,
Thoughts racing through my brain.

A friendly smile,
White angel's style,
She calms my inner fear.
Into a room,
You'll see him soon,
She whispers in my ear.

So still so sweet,
Those tiny feet,
You'd make my life complete.
I stand and stare,
Afraid to care,
Lest life be short and sweet.

That tiny form,
So snug and warm,
A fragile butterfly.
Still holding on,
A will so strong,

Not ready yet to die.

I cannot touch,
But love so much,
Please hear my silent pleas.
This heart breaking,
These arms aching,
My body ill at ease.

As time drags by,
I laugh I cry,
But now the dye is cast.
I touch your face,
A sweet embrace,
Now mine to hold at last.

Just look at you,
Still shining through,
Performing quite a feat.
A promise gave,
Your life to save,
No bitter, just the sweet.

Margaret Grant

COMA

Flowers on my windowsill
Pale and lifeless, cut
And steeped in old water
Their heads shun the light.
The scent of the lilies
Streaks my mind, lost
As it is in memories
With no hope of return.
This bed, my soft grave,
White as the skin
Which papers my bones,
Holds a memory alone.

Rachael Spellman

KIDULTHOOD

That no-man's-land which lies in between.
No longer a child yet no closer to adulthood.
Floating amidst an uncertain sea,
Of strange emotions and changes,
Willing to understand, to belong,
Hoping that one day you will break out of your cocoon,
A beautiful person recognised in your own right.
An independent, uninfluenced, free individual.
But for now the torrents of unexplained feelings,
Which toss you from one mood to the next,
Overcome your very being creating instability,
Uncertainty and the fear of the unknown.
It's a dangerous place . . . kidulthood.
Too old to be spoon fed,
Yet too young to walk the world alone.
Through the dusty tunnel of life you venture,
Stumbling yet never falling.
Searching blind for that which you cannot obtain.
Never clearly defined, never truly relatable.
Forever a mystery.

Charlotte Crisp

TO SEE THE TRUTH

From eyes to my mind
there is time
for correction.
This is not the truth,
two perspectives
melting into compromise.
A cyclops doesn't lie.
An eye for an eye
comes to mind.
There is time
to find truth
before I put on
my glasses.

Ina Schroders-Zeeders

NETWORKING NOT WORKING

I've sipped my tea then let it fester
Now I search in vain for a Wrigleys Extra
The seminar's over but I'm stuck to my seat
Preferring death to the 'meet and greet'

Just how does 'one' learn to talk shop
stop . . . (look, listen)
then thoughtfully digest?
Press the flesh
feign genuine interest
In a range of subjects I loathe and detest
Sparkle (effervesce)
Then work the room like a stale breath sex pest

You're oozing B eau as you move through the room
Your pink shirt and pin stripes pre-ordained in the womb
Your hairline
your iPhone
your chin like a shoe
Still when I grow up I'd like to be you

Stephen Quinlan

HALF HIDDEN

On solitary nights when the moon is half hidden
I waltz in the thoughts of fears bedridden,
Tucked away and forgotten!
I lavish myself with joys ill-gotten.
Those lil' pleasures of sinners God's forgotten.
I sip my champagne on grass dew-stricken,
And sigh the release of trophies I've forsaken.

On solitary nights when the moon is half hidden,
I tango with a blackened conscience
All the while smiling wryness devoid of innocence.
Half way between contentment and insanity
I kiss the stars and they wink back reassuringly.
For they see the others beneath their skies
That will this honesty but instead choose a disguise!

Hannah Nanyanzi

A WELCOMING

Come rain, Come shine
We'll welcome you
Come rain, Come shine
There's always a view
Come rain, Come shine
The pier's still grand
Come rain, Come shine
We'll have a band
Come rain, Come shine
There's plenty to do
Come rain, Come shine
Seats wait for you
Come rain, Come shine
You can play the slots
Come rain, come shine
You could win a pot
Come rain, Come shine
There's fish and chips
Come rain, Come shine
And, flavoursome dips
Come rain, Come shine
We've Weston in rock
Come rain, Come shine
Just look in the shops
Come rain, Come shine
And, still there is lots
Come rain, Come shine
We'll welcome you

Peter G H Payne

SEA OF DREAMS

A constant dream of a sea of blue,
Is forever within my sleep.
Where the clearest surface lies flat on top,
With its floor a mile deep.
But beyond that sea I'll never know,
It remains a mystery within my mind.
For I wake each time I'm almost there,
So its secret I am yet to find.
But I imagine a place of beauty,
A place where Heaven shines its light.
Then lay down on that sandy beach,
And wait for the stars to fill the night.
A place where your heart can never be broken,
And your troubles just drift out to sea.
Where the only person that controls my life,
That decides my fate is me.
But across that beach is a stranger,
A shadow I long to meet.
Where the slightest thought just warms my heart,
To where I can no longer stand the heat.
But I have no choice but to wait and see,
As for now that's the way it seems.
But this place will always remain in my heart,
And be forever my sea of dreams.

A G Clark

FALLEN FOR NOTHING

(For those who fell and fought for us all)

I was the one there from the start,
I was the one that could not wait to take part,
I was the one that saw men fall apart,
I held England within my heart.

Four years on after death and decay,
We are home, heroes for a day,
Home in a land ravaged and torn,
A land of free speech for all to be born.

Two decades on I do it again,
As once more I fight in the King's name,
many more fallen, many more dead,
I am the man who witnessed this bloodshed.

Once again back home, I land on the shore,
back in a land ravaged by war,
Now I rebuild, erase battle scars,
I do this for my family so I may see them all go far.

Now I am old, time went so fast,
here I stand one of the last,
once in a land filled with pride,
I am the ex Tommy destroyed by what I find,
A land of free speech? I'm afraid that's not so,
so please will you tell me, why did but boys fall in war.

Vincent J Hewitt

MUMMY LOOK!

Look at her running and jumping,
Twirling and singing her sweet songs,
Look at the sun on her golden hair,
She's playing and I'm here watching her,
Sharing in all she sees, answering her questions
Mummy look!
Soon she'll be grown up and I'll sit here alone,
Thinking and remembering, wondering,
Did I give her enough of my time, enough attention.
If I had her from a little girl again would I do more?
How I'll wish to hear those sweet songs,
And see that hair blowing in the wind, shining in the sun.
Mummy, come and see!
How I'll wish I could just reach out and touch her,
Feel her little hand in mine, Oh how much I'll miss my little girl.
Look mummy, boatmen, blossoms, She says in that excited, gleeful voice,
As she scoops up blossom then face to the sky and arms high . . .
She throws them into the air, delighted,
As they fall on and around her.
Look Mummy, I'm a bride.
Being her mother is the most wonderful pleasure there is.
Look Mummy, come and see!
And I do, I take that outstretched hand and I hold on . . .

R Hoare-Bond

STARDUST

Looking out
Beyond the sun, the moon, its stars,
I ponder of love and its warm flesh,
Casting its roots into the earth,
Anchoring, and yet,
Like a fairy of a dandelion's clock,
Gently floating on the wind's soft curves,
And finally,
Settling in its warm nest at night.

And if I am conceived in love,
Is that breathed into my fragile heart,
In a single moment?
These feelings are weightless cannons:
Light of cells and blood,
But throb like heavy stones.

And should a lighter creature pass me by,
My bones will chime,
And garden for words, pondering for hours,
And hope that time will allow me this.

And when my body is but dust,
I muse that the stars will brighten,
And daffodils blossom,
For when this story is complete,
My love will ponder hence in meadows.

Victoria Knowles

MY PRAYER

Oh God! Our heavenly father,
Harken to my prayer.
Please give me one small sign
To know that you are there.

Help me be a better person,
The best that I can be.
Help me care more for others
Than I could ever care for me.

Let me understand how others feel
And help them all I can.
Let me be a good support
For my fellow man.

Let me find time to listen
When someone needs an ear.
Let me soothe and calm them
When they live in fear.

Let me be unselfish.
And give as much of me
As you gave, when you let
Your son die on that tree.

I've tried to live a good life
And when I'm laid to rest,
I hope it will be said of me
I tried my very best.

Farina May Jenkins

THE RIOTS: BE THE CHANGE

I saw something scary the other day
Like a demon sent from hell
That brought the lost generation to one consensus:
To kill and destroy . . .

They were thieves in the night
And they took more than a bite
They took people's homes and livelihoods
And took people's lives from their own hoods

For what? To feed their greed?
Destroy the hand that feeds?
Defecate on the land they need?

I mean what the heck happened?
It turned from a protest into grand theft
Automatically spread like a virus
We couldn't see
We didn't use our iris
We couldn't see the huge line that divides us
From the animals

They turned into sheep
They became followers
They couldn't think for themselves
So they became borrowers
Some bit off more than they could chew
And their faces were shown all over the news
Crying, because now they will lose their freedom
Guess you could call them losers

'Cause let's be real, this was not child's play
Yet I'm seeing 12-year-olds
That went out of their way
To rob up shops like it's a day job
And it spread like wildfire
I'm seeing Manchester and Birms on fire
People using twitter and BBM to conspire
Not against symbols of the state, like parliament or the banks
They looted their own community
Yeah that's smart, yeah, thanks (!)

Woah!
Did you ever imagine this happening?
Or are we too content in our own imaginings?
In a false sense of security
Being told assuredly

That it's over now, it's in the past
Cameron has sorted it and so we can't be asked
It wasn't my house burning, lighting up the dark
It wasn't my friends messing up the streets and the parks
It wasn't my finger that pulled that trigger
But what would you see, if you saw the bigger picture?

Would you see the negativity in our technology?
The violence in our music, games and TV
Or our budget-cutting confused MPs
Lying about expenses and closing libraries
When we need to read
To educate ourselves so that we can be free
From the manipulative powers that be

It's funny how the justice system seems to fail
And sentences aren't deterring the youths from jail
Parents who 'smack' get sent there as well
And these families are too broke to ever make bail
We live in a mad world
Daily the news says we live in a sad world

Like how 35,000 London children are living in poverty
But we don't live in a poor city
Sometimes the truth can be too gritty to swallow
So instead we bury our heads and remain hollow
Fixating on soaps and living in virtual realities
So engrossed in social networks and in our TVs
An addictive disease
Best believe they're there for a reason
To programme you until your due season

Because if we ever overcame our deepest fear
And became powerful beyond measure

Things would definitely have to change, and change for the better

August 2011 was crazy and should never repeat it self
Be the change and not the hindrance; let's better ourselves.

Rochelle 'Rochelle LoRo' Logan-Rodgers

WHAT IS THE POINT IN LIFE

Every Second,
Every Minute,
Every Hour,
Of Every Day,
Is Slowly But Surely Ticking Away.

From Baby,
To Infant,
From Toddler,
To Child,
From Teenager,
To Adult.
Each Stage Lasts Just A While.

What Is The Point In Life?
To Lead You To God's Door?
Or To Go To Hell?
Where You'll Be Burned Once More?

Dianna Harman

BEYOND THE VALE

Beyond the vale
Beneath the scars
Beyond the void
Below the stars
A finest hour without encore
A rasp for breath as the curtain falls
As silence blasts from the seats and stalls
With discordant echoes from within the walls
Vibrations shudder foundations deep
As the stage below begins to creek
A fear long kept inside now creeps
To stir this slumbering beast from sleep
Soft voices sing a song so sweet
Though somewhere in the melody
A sombre tone begins to weep
As all start marching with the beat
Into a light I've never seen
A dream is all it's ever been

Mathew Pearce

SNOWDROPS

We've waited long enough
in this deep frozen winter,
more white than green or brown.
By degrees, our spirits dropped,
descending into deeply double figures,
below the point
at which we measure much at all.
It all seems pointless.

Dark and long,
the nights are never-ending.
Cold and short,
the days add little comfort.
Hard and lifeless,
the ground is like a grave.

And then, by stealth,
the mercury creeps upwards,
touching above zero.
The sky is now less grey,
the cloud a little higher,
the light a soft shade brighter.

The ground gives way
a fraction; the grass,
and green, emerges,
setting the scene
for buried battalions
of tiny shoots – and then they come:
the magic, maiden flowers,
silent heralds of renewal.

But listen to this silence.
It is an exclamation.
Choir upon choir
of snowdrops,
singing.

In celebration.

Gordon Hutchins

THE DANCE

Without you
I wouldn't have a clue,
And since the moon would be always blue,
I'd probably sit round wondering who next to sue;
A week is seven days too long,
The birds no longer break out into song
And I get all my mental arithmetic wrong;
The stars no longer come out to shine
And I can't tell a satsuma from a clementine
Let alone a koala from a kangaroo.

Without you
I wonder what I did before
You appeared and swept me off that floor;
Did I ever tie my shoe laces up?
Did I drink from a beaker, mug or cup?
Did I tidy knives and forks in their appropriate drawer?
Might my clothes be discovered on a lone seashore?
I probably put my feet up and smoked
A dozen cigars that made me choke,
Or downed ten malts at thrice the rate
It takes a man to become inebriate.

Without you
I lost tax receipts for my year-end return,
Confused the Battle of Bosworth with Bannockburn
Had different times set on all my clocks,
Forgot where I'd put my box of odd socks
And couldn't tell my hebes from my hollyhocks.

Without you
I'd only be half a man
With the other half packed off in a little yellow van
Blindfolded and lost without fieldmap or compass
Blundering through life in an unseemly rumpus.
I'd suffer a complete loss of confidence
Not be able to tell a cox from a conference
And when I mistook a berberis for a bougainvillea
Well, things couldn't get any sillier.

But with you
My garden comes into flower
A week passes quicker than an hour
The meaning of life is contained in a dance
Which witnesses us dancing all over France
Extending to a cafe in 'gay Paree'
Where we'd continue to celebrate that most unmagnetic fact
That like poles do actually attract
And that this knowledge has set us free.

Richard Haynes

APOCALYPTIC SLIDE

Darkness covers polluted lands, where death and squalor reside,
for our eternal battle with mother earth, this apocalyptic slide.
our constant rape of nature's gifts, our technological advance,
has obliterated landscapes, proffered no second chance.
our suicidal ignorance, whilst tearing down the trees,
our blinded sense of reality, as we poison global seas.
we plunder and we ravage for fuel and mineral ore,
we digest and rot this planet, down to its very core.
pestilence and famine, catastrophes and war,
the reason for these insane acts, I can't recall what for.
why ignorance for wisdom, why suicide for life,
why inflict this Armageddon, this intolerance and strife.
this living hellish vision, that humanity has made,
a sunless, bird less empty world, no tree or grassy blade,
one thing is all we have now, our imagination of what was,
an Eden of gods given earth, perfection with no flaws.
a doorway to past lifetimes, when mother nature once more lived,
when she nurtured man and animal, with her priceless precious gift.

James Howden

TERMINATION (IN PROGRESS)

Outcast to the depths of hell
These are the dark places that they dwell
Encased in hate and immersed in fear
Climbing the walls of this cylindrical sphere

Termination has become the norm
Intricate manipulation on a dissipated nation
Through self deprecation and aggravation
Bow down and let your life deform

In the shadows they prey
Sneaking, reeking
Seeking and destroying
Until it's judgement day

Weaving in and out of time
Victimless of a paraless crime
Interrupting the balance
Serving with the deepest of malice

Termination is what we prepare for
Through these implements of civil war
Stripped back for termination and installation
Subtly enjoying perverse mental misappropriation

Darkness falls, abstract light
Shrieking of lungs fills this night
Deviate from the human norm
Chaos is flowing within me
Take up the terminated form

Bones breaking, metal adjusting
Begin encrusting!

The sound of death fills the air
Black masks and evil eyes are added
This world has had it
Prepare to submit

Let the termination begin!

Rob Amos

WHY AM I STARING AT YOU?

My feet are too mite,
To ramble the journey called life.
The fingers of my hands are puny,
To touch and paint the world of beauty.

My vision is limited,
Its focused is only world-minded.
My body is frail,
Afraid to go down the rail.

Not yet ready to go fast,
To compete the fast growing society in a rush.

Why I am staring at you?
Because I find the person in you,
Who can help and guide me
To get my way.

You have explorable feet
who can walk with me on my journey.
You have long fingers in your hands
that touches the beauty of nature
Open hands that are always ready
to catch me when I fall.

You have strong body
to defend me when I am in trouble.
Your views are broad
that allows me to show
all the corners of the world.

You have courageous HEART
who can support me
when I'm feeling down & disturbed.

Why I am staring at you?
Because I wanted you to know
that I highly need you!

Fe T. Paglinawan-Gutierrez

HEDGEHOG

Pungent smell of earth, dirty,
Meaningless existence,
Overlooked, but under your nose,
Fleas. Who would touch? Who would appreciate?
Not me you would say.
Dirty, horrible things,
No point to them, not a second glance,
Lurking in the places you wouldn't be.
Muddy.
A diet of worms, slugs and all things horrid.

Not worthy.
Put a stick in it.
Kick it about; have some fun,
Run it over; ha ha!
No feeling; no life,
Who would miss it?
Who cares?
Stinky creature; unattractive prickles;
Poor excuse for a tail!

Who would care? Who would miss it?

Rare.
Beautiful, sweet, cute,
Just take a look,
Unique, exquisite, declined,
Pretty black eyes, all knowing and wise,
Wet, little nose. They smell you too!
They hear all,
Inquisitive but shy,
They feel, they hurt, they think,
They suffer, they go hungry,
Elusive, night time visitors.
A privilege, a pleasure,
Scared and needy,
Their dwindling numbers, everyone counts.
They live with us, around us, under our noses.

They need our protection, our understanding,
Our help to go on living,
Not our help to go on dying.
Cherish each one, not torture it,
Love not loathe,
Help not hinder,
Let live not kill.
Be human not an animal.
Show compassion, not ignorance.

Jane Wingfield

ON THE RED LIGHT

The consummate professional:
Chatting, to put me at my ease.
Gently he helps me to prepare:
Attentive – then deftly prompting,
Questioning – polishing my speech.

And I feel fine: with thoughts marshalled,
My favourite phrases practised, checked,
I'm eloquent and in control.

'I think we're ready now,' he says,
'*We're rolling when the red light shows.'*

And on the red light thoughts escape,
Eloquence evaporates as
I become a stuttering wreck –
Tongue almost tied . . .

Always on the
Red light it's the same: confidence
Withers, lines are fluffed, the simplest
Truth stays lodged in my dry throat.
Always at these times I need my best –
Instead, thick tongued, I croak, whisper
All of life's most important lines
Like . . . '*I love you, love you, love you.'*

Patrick B Osada

LILITH

I keep the secret of my love
In bitter sting and blue cold light,
And how She comes not from above
To chase the low perpetual night;
From whence She comes I do not tell,
Of her existence nobody knows,
Or how She brings the Flowers of Hell
To place with my one sickened Rose.

I sit in silence as I will
In private as the Stars begin
To rise on all that slumbers still,
Until She wakes me with her Sin;
My secret bitch comes as the Sun
Sets on the jagged granite rocks
And as the blood and venom run
She arises from her coffin box.

I keep her quiet She soothes the pain
Of burning waters on my brow,
She hides me from the caustic rain
That saturates the soil of Now;
Our union of this place is not
And knows no land or vista here,
Black and scarlet bright and hot
She comes to decimate The Fear.

I keep her safely as I should
Away from all your prying eyes,
And in the dark She sucks my blood
From out of all that slowly dies;
In blazing passion we enmesh
And frost becalms my ribboned heart
That worships all Unholy Flesh
Whose rapture shall not now depart.

I keep the vigil of the brave
And tremble as She holds my hand
That wants me for a nameless grave
Should I explore the shadow land;
Her crimson and ethereal gaze
Turns quick my pallid skin to stone,
Yet with her I must share my days
Or die in agony and alone.

I keep my love for her in shade
Exalted in the word unsaid,
Her touch is of Infinity's Blade
So I join not the many dead;
Of Fire and Ice is her caress
That makes and also doth destroy,
And yet within her darkest dress
She gives to me the Food of Joy.

I keep her bosom close to mine
And drink deep of her suicide
That comes from off the acid vine
When She runs hot and free inside;
Within the chill of her embrace
She numbs my agony with her kiss
And takes me from an ugly place
To love me in the Great Abyss.

I keep her bitter loving arms
Around me for the Dread Desire
To be kept from the light that harms
She floods me with unending fire;
My lover Lilith licks the chains
And gives to me Eternal Breath,
Her passion running in my veins,
She saves me from the Second Death.

I keep the secret I adore,
In boiling ecstasy She prevails
A wanton wild and fearsome Whore
Who tears my flesh with iron nails;
I go to her in nauseous grief
That only She can truly heal
Because She knows of my Belief
And of the way I truly feel.

Barry Mac

PIECE BY PIECE

Around me lies on every hand,
A foreign place: my native land.
So little's left of what I knew –
Of places, friends and things we'd do.
Is this the town where I began,
And lived as child and youth and man?
All tar and glass and painted lines –
Don't Stop; Pay Here; Obey the Signs!
The market hall's a car park now;
An office block, The Horse and Plough;
The few shops left, a car-free row
Where those disabled may not go.
And gone, the haunts of childhood play
Where once we'd pass the summer day:
The wood, the brook, the ruined mill,
The disused quarry on the hill . . .
You hear no children's laughter now
From mill or brook or oaken bough;
The Health and Safety man has been,
And all are banished from the scene.
Yet all restored could not assuage
The inward ravages of age.
I cannot run to catch a train,
Nor mount a roof to clear a drain,
While yonder hills, so easy won
When heart and lung and limb were young,
Deny me but their gentlest few –
Whence dimming eyes befog the view.
The friends with whom I'd work and play
And take a jar at close of day,
Now, one by one, they turn away:
Some turn to ashes, some to clay.
And one above them all I miss,
No longer here to hold or kiss,
Nor even see, except in sleep.
Her memory alone, I keep.
I linger on. My years accrue,
Each midnight bringing yet a day,
While all the world I ever knew
Is taken, piece by piece, away.

Thomas Ryland

I HATE MORNINGS ALL OVER AGAIN (AND I'M OKAY WITH THAT)

So I guess now that the hole isn't so jagged
And my voice doesn't break into a hush
On the second syllable of your name
Like I'm awestruck and not
Heartbroken (and shamed)
It must mean I'm ready to wake up one day
And forget about you

And now every day is a list of all the things
You didn't do and didn't say
A wake-up call every time I think about
Everything I gave up and lost
Through ego (and doubt)
And I'm learning to hate the mornings again
Like I did before you came

But sometimes I have these thoughts of you
That I just can't box away for good
Because they belong to me and you and this
And you are mine, in a way
To remember (and miss)
And why should I forget the girl that I was
When I thought I was yours

And it was okay to walk with a spring in my step
Remembering the nights that came before
Like the heat of your hand on my thigh
And curling myself inward, into you
With a smile (and a sigh)
Because it wasn't worth it, with you
To be cold and brittle and hard

But I'm growing tired of the effort it takes
To remind myself constantly to forget and forget
And I'm ready to look back now and say
'I can't believe the bad poetry I wrote
About those early days!'
And I'll laugh and laugh so hard it will hurt
And it'll seem so easy then, how I learned to forget

Lianne Lee

SKIN

I like your skin
I want to trace my nose upon your cheeks
And breathe in your faint fat smell and the milk
And where your neck is creased
Where the warmth of babyhood nestles
I want to touch lightly that skin
New and blossomed
Unmarked, without freckles or shades
Unique all over
Growing and pink
White and clean
You in your skin.

Gillian Lawrence

MOTHER TO MY MOTHER

How did I become you mother?
When you were the one that carried me for nine months.
Why did I end up caring for you, when you're the one that lays down with my dad?
Why is it I'm your cook, your cleaner, carer and financer but just about your daughter?
How is it so, I've mopped up your sick?
Cleaned up your shit, looked after your kids.
Why did I spend my life doing your job, waiting for you to come home, lock doors and put lights out?
Shouting, dictating, giving you the speech about life and the company you keep.
How is it so, twenty years have passed, but I'm still fixing your mistakes in the past.
Warning you about the men you see, and mistakes you forever continue to make.
When I visit you, why do I leave with my purse light?
Lending you money that I never get back, to support your fag habit and maintain your electric and gas.
Explain to me the logic, the science in how this works?
If you gave birth to me
And I am meant to be your child
Then why have we spent life the other way round.
And even now when I have my own child
I gave birth to one child but still I have lots.
Our roles have still yet to be reverse
The responsibility still remains
I am still a mother to my mother, not her daughter or her child.

Rieanna Wilkinson

FOR LACHLAN

You came here for a little while,
Long enough to make me smile,
Long enough to make me see,
How precious being a mum can be.
I can still remember your little ways
How you brightened boring days
When you flung your arms around my neck
And snuggled in whilst we watched Shrek.
The many books we read together,
I thought I'd have you until forever
But in a breath you slipped away
Despite me willing you to stay.
In a whisper you just disappeared
Leaving behind a trail of tears
An empty bed, a painful silence
Emotions raw with grief and violence
Toys abandoned, no longer used
A mothers mind lost and confused.
Now although it's nine years on,
Your spirit remains, tho' your body's gone.
I think of you when a rainbow appears
When a song is played from the 'Lachlan years'.
When I set free a helium balloon
And the dream works boy who sits in the moon.
Blowing bubbles and Gingermen
Love you to the moon and back again
Your siblings and I discuss you often
And over the years the pain does soften.
But today I remember the day we parted
The day you left me broken-hearted
There is a part of me that died that day,
When I begged you not to drift away,
You came here for just a little while,
But the memories you left still make me smile.

Maria Lawton

FLAG WAVING: A POEM FOR THE 6TH OF JUNE

At H-Hour on D-Day an Armada of liberty
Brought men and women of flesh, blood
And bones and many countries to the
Wide open sands of Normandy.
And so began a day of death, of violence,
Of fear and bravery and of unity.

An armada built out of a treaty of
Trades unionists and industrialists;
Carrying painters, paper hangers,
Lathe turners and bankers, mechanics
And pastry chefs, dustmen and postmen,
Managers and workers, shirkers and
Farm labourers who ran up those
Beaches on that wet June day.

Facing Nazi bullets and mortars
Which drew no distinction between
Lords and Knights or miners and steelworkers.
Long barrelled guns cut down double-barrelled names.
And the Georges, the Alfies, the Charlies
And the Tommies, that day of days, all the same.

Sword, Gold, Utah, Omaha and Juno,
Stretches of bloody sand where men of
All ranks and class became a brotherly band
And got on with the job in hand of
Staying alive and continuing the people's
Stand against the 45 degree raised hand
And the stupidity and banality of the Nazi Klan.

Where to a woman and a man in planes,
On the sea, in the factories and on the land
Defiance against fascism was writ large
In a battle plan named Overlord.

And for those murderers of Jews, Gypsies,
Homosexuals and the Disabled the legions
From many nations on board those ships
Brought a reckoning forged by unity and justice.

The 6th of June, 1944 was the biggest
Seaborne invasion the world ever saw;
But not an invasion for riches, mineral wealth
Or money, an invasion by those who refused
To surrender to an evil, despotic tyranny.

And for all those barbers and bus drivers who
Ran up those beaches that day, it's for you
And your comrades I'll wave a flag for any day.

And I thank you all from my Albion born,
Internationalist heart.

Bob Hill

TIME PASSES

At eighteen
free and full of fun
I thought
at thirty life was done.
By thirty I was
in my prime
I never seemed to
have the time
to wonder
how my life would be
if I ever got
to sixty-three
Sixty-nine I soon will be!
That girl of eighteen
Lives in me.
My heart remains
still young and free
I thank my God
That I am me.

Kathleen Hoare

THE HISTORY OF JIM JAM THE CURTAIN CAT

Before Nineteen Seventy Five,
When my childhood was well established and alive
You used to hang there day and night
Sometimes shading
The bright
Sun given
Light
So that the newly coloured television screen
Could be clearly seen

But since that date
Of which I write
You have gained
A new life
That no longer has any
Pulling or drawing strife

Your straight, yet folded edges,
Became an orange and brown
Swirly,
Whirly,
Patterned coat,
In which,
If you were alive,
You would stalk and sleep
Amongst roadside hedges.

With needle and thread,
And motherly care
With oodles of love,
There's plenty both here
And there
To share

With added
Hope and luck
You were given,
Legs,
Tail,
Head,
Ears and eyes
As well as a love sewn
Smile,
That smile would accompany me on
Each and every school bound mile

Your zippered belly,
Now remains empty,
But in those days gone by,
When my spirits weren't always high
Your stomach
Was a home
Alone
To my night-time wear
Where they in their many patterned designs
Were kept warm,
Warm and cosy
Like my memories and feelings
Conjured up by two words,
One term,
'Family home',

I gave you your name,
Which has been uttered again and again
I call you 'Jim Jam'
Because, in years gone by,
During my waking hours,
Your zippered belly,
Were home, warmth and security,
To my very own Jim Jams,

With memories stored,
Moments shared,
We have both moved on,
Unseparated,
Together,
Forever,
Endlessly
Unceasingly linked
With my present and future
Family.

Neill Cadmore

NO MORE TEARS RUN DOWN MY CHINA FACE

I have a dream – to live my life.
A future as a mother and wife.
It's not much to ask, it's only small.
It won't change the world at all!

So why am I used like a doll made of china?
Just an object with no feeling inside her?
I watched as if imprisoned inside,
As slowly the dream faded and dies!

My heart aches, bleeds and screams,
The pain endured by my shattered dreams,
Why am I continually put to one side?
Causing pain – I find – impossible to hide!

The tears slide down my china face,
I try to cover with kindness and grace,
I treat all the people I meet the same,
Most of them just return with pain.

So now it's time to stand on my feet,
To face the world whatever I meet,
To stop the tears, and find the place
That puts a smile on my china face!

To create a world where my dreams come true,
Where love and sunshine comes shining through,
To show them all I can stand tall,
No more trying to fight against them all,

I'll take a break, restore my heart,
Make a happy healthy brand new start,
I'll keep the kindness, and the grace.
Put on a smile, find my happy place.

I'll face them all – proud and tall.
No longer tiny, invisible and small,
I'll watch as life slowly picks up the pace!
No more tears down my china face!

No more will I take the constant flak,
It's time to start fighting back,
Time to find a brand new task,
So I can get rid of this china mask.

So my personality, hope and love shine through,
So I can have what I am due,
I'll be a wife and a mum, when the time is right.
To this end – I will fight.

I'll take away the target used,
As people think I'm to be abused,
I will have babies, love and lace,
No more tears down my China face.

Jennie May

SWEET, SICK, CINNAMON

Glossy under clinging raindrops,
Red and open like a wound.
Keys jangle, dangling from the lock.
My toes, they curl into mutton
Carpet as the door swings shut.
'What a day,' he says.
His nose is pink. His eyes are wary.
'What a day.'

Lifeless at the window where,
A radiator below burns my bare knees.
The world is ink and scattered pins.
Pools of amber flickering.
Liquid fireflies in orange and caramel
Struggling to stay afloat, slowly sinking.
Behind me, behind walls,
I hear creaking of weight on floorboards,
He calls to me. For me.

What a sad girl I am.

Veronique Falconer

PROUD PEOPLE UNITE

Proud to be myself
Oh yes I am

I am a much more beautiful person
Than you ever know. This is what I wished for

I wish I can stand up
And take a bow.

Let the world
Know that I am coming out
Of my shell.

Proud to be myself
Oh yes I am.

It is me who controls
My life

Who choose the right route

Hate is such a harsh word
Let's never hear that word any more.

I want more people to feel
Beautiful, powerful, strong

Let the whole world know
That you are coming out of
Your shell

Imogen Brand

YURI GARGARIN

I am the first man to leave Earth's orbit.
I'm feeling claustrophobic in this getup.
My legs do not belong to me.
Whose are these hands?
I am beyond my bones,
Beyond gravity.

My head feels fuzzy.
My wife is putting the baby
To bed down on the earth,
And the other half of the world
Is just awakening, reaching for
The razor, the paper, the coffee.

Wish I could do normal things
But I do not think I will
Be the same again.
They should send poets into space
Not cosmonauts, it's a waste
Of space.

When I return I'll be a hero,
I will drink too much.
I will get fat.
Who wants a fat
Cosmonaut?

I will have affairs, my
Wife will be ashamed of me,
I will jump out of a window
And fall on my head.

Brenda Liddy

OH, WHAT A PITY!

And such a case:
My star sometimes appears
And hurts my soul with its slanting eyes,
Or maybe I forever gaze at it,
And there is a sign of space between us,
A cast of silver rays for me to meet
The gloomy light and silence of the space.
Oh, what a case!

And such a case:
The Sun will give a kiss
And stir the whole world with blinding rounds,
Or maybe I feel giddy of the Sun
That tries its bloody swords with no bounds
And makes my lips be red and colours run
To those fields my Zodiac likes to graze.
Oh, what a case!

And such a pity:
My time is losing seconds
With every look I give to shining stars,
Or maybe stars forever drop the petals
And vanish in the depth of space with us
To make all our seconds being fatal
And sinking in the great infinity . . .
Oh, what a pity!

Natalia Gorodova

NOTE THE INSPIRATION

Awake pen, write those lovely words worth reading
Words I long to tell, words I am not yet aware of
The tingle in my fingers unable to produce
Overwhelm me with that sensational feeling
Blank notes still lie on my desk

Doubt is always present, run I dare you!
Run? Madness, self-doubt is inevitable for a poet
The incompletion of thoughts, creased paper
Hubris, an overestimation of talent possessed!

One needs insanity to write . . .
One needs sadness . . .
One needs inspiration

Submerged in an illusion of a temporary reality
Finally I see the imagined obsolete truth
Ignored on a floral saucer, crumbs of dreams
Sleep sweet misery, a clue is presented

Found in the process, the adored marked X
Scattering joy, a fanfare to the unknown
Unsorted dreams of heavenly bliss
A token, indeed a writers treasure to behold

On flourish and scribble filled notes, letters appear
Reconciled feelings, I found it, my inspiration.

Louise Lorentzon

LABYRINTH OF LOVE

In the black holes love is lost within withering
Multitude of relations, lustful entitled adoring
Love is a picture of whispers under the moon
Staggering breath of death throes is mistune
Note on blood red roses is object of affection
Paying for ill father's blood drip erupts tension
No lost wink, not a pique in clandestine courting
Umbrageous wife sleep if to nurse child's crying
Sacred unison now a fable meant to blight in qualm
Rendezvous, court settlements opted as lines of palm
Gold, nickels and lands, a price for eternal wedlock
If delinquent, damsel a bequest to charnel's dock
Words are spilled on papers, tears are shed on stories
Love now a tale to sell in markets, just one of lost glories
Veiled in arduous layers, hidden within integral part
Sacrifice , faith can sweep love from labyrinth's heart

Ayesha Zainab Beg

ON A RAINY DAY: A PARALLEL POEM

I open, you
Close, or you
Open, I
Close, either
My umbrella
Or yours

To keep
Both ourselves
Dry and warm
From this cold
Rain, we have
To share
The one
The same
Umbrella, if we
Must walk
Hand
In hand

Changming Yuan

FAMISHED FEMININITY

Lift the latch and
you will find cracks
in the door, scarred
traces of hot tempered
rackets –

sad sorrowful echoes of
screams slaps and strikes
in the tender dwellings of
famished femininity –

whose chest is crammed
with refrains of ugly curses
profane, drafted with hatred
mundane –

beauty's blend for care
created for eternal company
stays abused spared not -
why?

who will cut the strings
of human bondage
lacerant tortured
Suffering, Silent Cry!

What was ancient
ignorant and abolished -
made eloquent and sacred,

Open the door and you will find
famished femininity current
in countless fetters

slowly visibly tabescent –

Why –

Anjum Wasim Dar

TOXIC LOVE

You're the villain
You're the hero
Burns like fire
This forbidden desire
You're a beautiful bad
A good kind of sad
It's a tie
The stakes are high

You are too bad
You are too good
There is no cure
To your allure
I cannot repel
Your spell
Have you any clue
I hate that I love you

You feel so wrong
You feel so right
Can't fight this feeling
Can't stop this from happening
I cannot be saved
I am your slave
Take me
Have me

You are my devil
You are my angel
You win
You got under my skin
My heart's in prison
You had it poison
I am an addict
To your love so toxic

Tersia De Jager

THE EYES

She lost her dearest one
The one who gave her joy
The one who brought her sweetness
The one who touch her heart
The one who tugged her soul
Two hearts converge
And . . .
the image
the memory
stays forever

But the day of joy passed
No longer has its ray
No longer the warmth hug in through
The touch is just inside a memory
The kindness disappears
And compassion is only just imagination

It hurts her heart
It destroys her pure soul
Only the eyes she can remember
The soul of gentleness
The root of tenderness
She keeps the glare
She memorised the stare
And retains the beautiful moments
Before it fades away

She sees another glare
She knows that other stare
Where ever she moves
That eyes follow
She discerns the admiration
But nothing can change her mind
The first eyes will be the one
The first eyes will never apart
From her heart
From her soul
Evermore

Vashti Trisawati Abhidana

FAILURE TO INFLUENCE

There is madness to my method,
Yet a method to my madness;
And my method is the key
To my overflowing gladness.
But why do I say that I am glad?
When the other girls only think I'm mad?

They think I'm insane because I don't follow
The latest trends.
They think I'm mental because I don't follow
The latest brands.
They think I'm an imbecile because I don't follow
Their style and fashion.
They think I'm a lunatic because I don't follow
Their kind of passion.
But above all the nutty things of their world,
They think I'm an idiot because I don't follow
The popular girl.

Why can't I be different?
Why can't I be special?
Why can't I be unique?
Why can't I be exceptional?
Why can't the rest of them see
That I simply want to be me?
Not a star-struck wannabe
Or merely a mock copy
Of the girl who walks down the corridors
With a swaggering gait and a vainglorious smile
Flashing her thirty-two bleached teeth.
The crowd parts like a second Red Sea.

I will never be a martyr to influence
Because I'm aware of the consequence.
I won't listen to music that is not to my liking,
Wear the latest trends that are too revealing,
Act in a manner just to be appealing,
Or walk in a way that sends me reeling,
Just to blend in with the rest of the world,
Or rather to blend in with the popular girls.

Will I let them sway my personality?
Will I let them shake my confidence?
Will I let them mould my character?
Over my dead body.
Sometimes I have a grasping urge

To holler in their faces:
'I would rather be alone than to
Be an artificial clone of you.
I will never change the things I do,
Just to be like you.'

Emily Ho

THE POET AND THE PUSSY

A Great Man once said . . .

'Those who never experience
madness at least once in their lives
haven't lived'

I believe this to be true . . .

Once I was rummaging in a bin
for scraps, down town
and
I was tapped on the shoulder by a Cat

he was dressed head to toe in fur
I remember because it was a really hot day

He said
'save something for me, I'm starving'

I replied

'I hate my life,
There's more crap in it, than there is in this trash can'

I can't believe I shared that with a Cat!

With a sigh,

he replied . . .

'Well at least
When you're gone you're gone'

I've still got eight lives to bloody live . . .

Shirley Harrison

THE ROBIN

The robin's song
Once more we hear
The sweetest sound
To grace the morn
Of a winter's day
So bare and forlorn

Hopping daintily
From branch to branch
Its scarlet breast
In majestic dance
Doth a winter's day
So bleak, enhance

A ray of sunshine
In such austere terrain
No falling snow
Will e'er detain
On a winter's day
So dark and grey

S J Roberts Adam Crawley

BLUEBELLS IN THE WOOD

A carpet of blue beneath my feet
Bluebells swaying in the evening breeze
Butterflies dancing from flower to flower
Spreading their pollen as they flutter about
The ripple of the stream as it flows by
A drop of rain falls from above
Refreshing the bluebells in the wood
Dappled sunshine can be seen through the dense trees
Such a calm and wondrous sight
Gazing at the bluebells in the wood

Doreen Cawley

FORWARD POETRY INFORMATION

We hope you have enjoyed reading this book - and that you will continue to enjoy it in the coming years.

If you like reading and writing poetry drop us a line, or give us a call, and we'll send you a free information pack.

Alternatively if you would like to order further copies of this book or any of our other titles, then please give us a call or log onto our website at www.forwardpoetry.co.uk.

Forward Poetry Information
Remus House
Coltsfoot Drive
Peterborough
PE2 9BF
(01733) 890099